A GIFT FOR

_____

FROM

_____

DATE

_____

BIBLE PRAYERS

TO GUIDE YOUR LIFE

JACK COUNTRYMAN

An Imprint of Thomas Nelson Publishers

THOMAS NELSON
Since 1798

ISBN 978-1-4002-4197-2 (audiobook)
ISBN 978-1-4002-4194-1 (eBook)
ISBN 978-1-4002-4183-5 (HC)

Printed in India

23 24 25 26 27 REP 10 9 8 7 6 5 4 3 2 1

CONTENTS

INTRODUCTION

The Bible is filled with everything you would want to know about leading a prayerful life. With scripture on topics such as prayer promises, preparation for prayer, and attitude and conditions for prayer, you will find what God's Word reveals about prayer.

Jeremiah 33:3 says, "Call to Me and I will answer you, and tell you [and even show you] great and mighty things, [things which have been confined and hidden], which you do not know and understand and cannot distinguish" (AMP). This book has been designed to open your mind and heart to God's Word and to show how much God wants us to communicate with Him through prayer. Our hope is that this book will touch your life in such a way that you will have a deeper relationship with our heavenly Father. He is waiting patiently for us to come to Him in prayer. May this book be a blessing to you as you deepen your prayer life.

AMAZING ANSWERS
TO PRAYER

In this portion of the book, we will explore how twenty-three characters in the Bible cried out to God and how He answered their prayers. This section clearly demonstrates how much God wants us to communicate with Him in prayer. We belong to the Father, and He wishes to interact with us in our daily lives.

As you read through these answered prayers, open your mind and heart to communicate with the Savior. He is waiting for you and wants to answer your prayers and live in the center of your life. The Holy Spirit has promised to guide us in a deeper prayer life. As the psalmist says in Psalm 19:14, "Let the words of my mouth and the meditation of my heart be acceptable in Your sight, O LORD, my strength and my Redeemer."

ABRAHAM

Prayer: Abraham for a child

Abram said, "Lord GOD, what will You give me, seeing I go childless, and the heir of my house is Eliezer of Damascus?" . . . Then He brought him outside and said, "Look now toward heaven, and count the stars if you are able to number them." And He said to him, "So shall your descendants be."

And he believed in the LORD, and He accounted it to him for righteousness.

GENESIS 15:2, 5–6

Answer

The LORD visited Sarah as He had said, and the LORD did for Sarah as He had spoken. For Sarah conceived and bore Abraham a son in his old age, at the set time of which God had spoken to him. And Abraham called the name of his son who was born to him—whom Sarah bore to him—Isaac.

GENESIS 21:1–3

Prayer: Abraham intercedes for Sodom

Abraham came near and said, "Would You also destroy the righteous with the wicked? Suppose there were fifty righteous within the city; would You also destroy the place and not spare it for the fifty righteous that were in it? Far be it from You to do such a thing as this, to slay the righteous with the wicked, so that the righteous should be as the wicked; far be it from You! Shall not the Judge of all the earth do right?"

So the LORD said, "If I find in Sodom fifty righteous within the city, then I will spare all the place for their sakes."

Then Abraham answered and said, "Indeed now, I who am but dust and ashes have taken it upon myself to speak to the Lord: Suppose there were five less than the fifty righteous; would You destroy all of the city for lack of five?"

So He said, "If I find there forty-five, I will not destroy it."

And he spoke to Him yet again and said, "Suppose there should be forty found there?"

So He said, "I will not do it for the sake of forty."

Then he said, "Let not the Lord be angry, and I will speak: Suppose thirty should be found there?"

So He said, "I will not do it if I find thirty there."

And he said, "Indeed now, I have taken it upon

myself to speak to the Lord: Suppose twenty should be found there?"

So He said, "I will not destroy it for the sake of twenty."

Then he said, "Let not the Lord be angry, and I will speak but once more: Suppose ten should be found there?"

And He said, "I will not destroy it for the sake of ten." So the Lord went His way as soon as He had finished speaking with Abraham; and Abraham returned to his place.

GENESIS 18:23–33

Answer

And it came to pass, when God destroyed the cities of the plain, that God remembered Abraham, and sent Lot out of the midst of the overthrow, when He overthrew the cities in which Lot had dwelt.

GENESIS 19:29

Prayer: Abraham's confidence in God

Abraham said, "My son, God will provide for Himself the lamb for a burnt offering." So the two of them went together.

GENESIS 22:8

Answer

Then Abraham lifted his eyes and looked, and there behind him was a ram caught in a thicket by its horns. So Abraham went and took the ram, and offered it up for a burnt offering instead of his son.

GENESIS 22:13

Prayer: Abraham prays for Isaac's wife

So Abraham said to the oldest servant of his house, who ruled over all that he had, "Please, put your hand under my thigh, and I will make you swear by the LORD, the God of heaven and the God of the earth, that you will not take a wife for my son from the daughters of the Canaanites, among whom I dwell; but you shall go to my country and to my family, and take a wife for my son Isaac."

GENESIS 24:2–4

Answer

Here is Rebekah before you; take her and go, and let her be your master's son's wife, as the LORD has spoken.

GENESIS 24:51

JACOB

Prayer: Jacob prays for deliverance

Then Jacob said, "O God of my father Abraham and God of my father Isaac, the LORD who said to me, 'Return to your country and to your family, and I will deal well with you': . . . Deliver me, I pray, from the hand of my brother, from the hand of Esau; for I fear him, lest he come and attack me and the mother with the children."

GENESIS 32:9, 11

Answer

"For You said, 'I will surely treat you well, and make your descendants as the sand of the sea, which cannot be numbered for multitude.'"

GENESIS 32:12

RACHEL

Prayer: Rachel prays for a child

Now when Rachel saw that she bore Jacob no children, Rachel envied her sister, and said to Jacob, "Give me children, or else I die!"

And Jacob's anger was aroused against Rachel,

and he said, "Am I in the place of God, who has withheld from you the fruit of the womb?"

GENESIS 30:1–2

Answer

Then God remembered Rachel, and God listened to her and opened her womb. And she conceived and bore a son, and said, "God has taken away my reproach." So she called his name Joseph, and said, "The LORD shall add to me another son."

GENESIS 30:22–24

ISRAEL

Prayer: Israel cries for deliverance
Now it happened in the process of time that the king of Egypt died. Then the children of Israel groaned because of the bondage, and they cried out; and their cry came up to God because of the bondage.

EXODUS 2:23

Answer

So God heard their groaning, and God remembered His covenant with Abraham, with Isaac, and with

Jacob. And God looked upon the children of Israel, and God acknowledged them.

EXODUS 2:24–25

MOSES

Prayer: Moses prays for grace

Remember Abraham, Isaac, and Israel, Your servants, to whom You swore by Your own self, and said to them, "I will multiply your descendants as the stars of heaven; and all this land that I have spoken of I give to your descendants, and they shall inherit it forever."

EXODUS 32:13

Answer

Nevertheless He regarded their affliction,
    When He heard their cry;
    And for their sake He remembered His
        covenant,
    And relented according to the multitude of His
        mercies.

PSALM 106:44–45

Prayer: Moses prays for glory

And he said, "Please, show me Your glory."

EXODUS 33:18

Answer

Then He said, "I will make all My goodness pass before you, and I will proclaim the name of the Lord before you. I will be gracious to whom I will be gracious, and I will have compassion on whom I will have compassion."

EXODUS 33:19

Prayer: Moses prays for the scattering of enemies

So they departed from the mountain of the Lord on a journey of three days; and the ark of the covenant of the Lord went before them for the three days' journey, to search out a resting place for them. And the cloud of the Lord was above them by day when they went out from the camp.

So it was, whenever the ark set out, that Moses said:

"Rise up, O Lord!
Let Your enemies be scattered,
And let those who hate You flee before You."

And when it rested, he said:

"Return, O Lord,
To the many thousands of Israel."

NUMBERS 10:33–36

Answer

Now when the people complained, it displeased the Lord; for the Lord heard it, and His anger was aroused. So the fire of the Lord burned among them, and consumed some in the outskirts of the camp. Then the people cried out to Moses, and when Moses prayed to the Lord, the fire was quenched.

NUMBERS 11:1–2

JOSHUA

Prayer: Joshua—That the sun stand still

Then Joshua spoke to the Lord in the day when the Lord delivered up the Amorites before the children of Israel, and he said in the sight of Israel:

"Sun, stand still over Gibeon;
And Moon, in the Valley of Aijalon."

JOSHUA 10:12

Answer

So the sun stood still,

And the moon stopped,

Till the people had revenge

Upon their enemies.

Is this not written in the Book of Jasher? So the sun stood still in the midst of heaven, and did not hasten to go down for about a whole day.

JOSHUA 10:13

SAMSON

Prayer: Samson prays for strength

Then Samson called to the LORD, saying, "O LORD GOD, remember me, I pray! Strengthen me, I pray, just this once, O God, that I may with one blow take vengeance on the Philistines for my two eyes!"

JUDGES 16:28

Answer

And Samson took hold of the two middle pillars which supported the temple, and he braced himself against them, one on his right and the other on his left. Then Samson said, "Let me die with the

Philistines!" And he pushed with all his might, and the temple fell on the lords and all the people who were in it. So the dead that he killed at his death were more than he had killed in his life.

JUDGES 16:29-30

GIDEON

Prayer: Gideon prays for a fleece

Then Gideon said to God, "Do not be angry with me, but let me speak just once more: Let me test, I pray, just once more with the fleece; let it now be dry only on the fleece, but on all the ground let there be dew."

JUDGES 6:39

Answer

And God did so that night. It was dry on the fleece only, but there was dew on all the ground.

JUDGES 6:40

MANOAH

Prayer: Manoah prays for his child

God listened to the voice of Manoah, and the Angel of God came to the woman again as she was sitting in the field; but Manoah her husband was not with her.

JUDGES 13:9

Answer

It happened as the flame went up toward heaven from the altar—the Angel of the LORD ascended in the flame of the altar! When Manoah and his wife saw this, they fell on their faces to the ground. . . . So the woman bore a son and called his name Samson; and the child grew, and the LORD blessed him.

JUDGES 13:20, 24

HANNAH

Prayer: Hannah asks for Samuel

She was in bitterness of soul, and prayed to the LORD and wept in anguish. Then she made a vow and said, "O LORD of hosts, if You will indeed look on the affliction of Your maidservant and remember me, and not forget Your maidservant, but will give Your maidservant a male child, then I will give him to the LORD all the days of his life, and no razor shall come upon his head."

1 SAMUEL 1:10–11

Answer

So it came to pass in the process of time that Hannah conceived and bore a son, and called his name Samuel, saying, "Because I have asked for him from the Lord."

1 SAMUEL 1:20

DAVID

Prayer: David kills Goliath

Then David said to the Philistine, "You come to me with a sword, with a spear, and with a javelin. But I come to you in the name of the Lord of hosts, the God of the armies of Israel, whom you have defied."

1 SAMUEL 17:45

Answer

So David prevailed over the Philistine with a sling and a stone, and struck the Philistine and killed him. But there was no sword in the hand of David.

1 SAMUEL 17:50

ELIJAH

Prayer: Elijah prays for fire

Hear me, O LORD, hear me, that this people may know that You are the LORD God, and that You have turned their hearts back to You again.

1 KINGS 18:37

Answer

Then the fire of the LORD fell and consumed the burnt sacrifice, and the wood and the stones and the dust, and it licked up the water that was in the trench.

1 KINGS 18:38

ELISHA

Prayer: Elisha prays for Shunammite's son

When Elisha came into the house, there was the child, lying dead on his bed. He went in therefore, shut the door behind the two of them, and prayed to the LORD.

2 KINGS 4:32–33

Answer

He returned and walked back and forth in the house, and again went up and stretched himself out on him;

then the child sneezed seven times, and the child opened his eyes.

2 KINGS 4:35

JABEZ

Prayer: Jabez prays for blessing
And Jabez called on the God of Israel saying, "Oh, that You would bless me indeed, and enlarge my territory, that Your hand would be with me, and that You would keep me from evil, that I may not cause pain!"

1 CHRONICLES 4:10

Answer
So God granted him what he requested.

1 CHRONICLES 4:10

JEROBOAM

Prayer: King Jeroboam asks for healing
Then the king answered and said to the man of God, "Please entreat the favor of the LORD your God, and pray for me, that my hand may be restored to me."

1 KINGS 13:6

Answer

So the man of God entreated the Lord, and the king's hand was restored to him, and became as before.

1 KINGS 13:6

HEZEKIAH

Prayer: Hezekiah prays for healing

Then he turned his face toward the wall, and prayed to the Lord, saying, "Remember now, O Lord, I pray, how I have walked before You in truth and with a loyal heart, and have done what was good in Your sight." And Hezekiah wept bitterly.

2 KINGS 20:2–3

Answer

"Return and tell Hezekiah the leader of My people, 'Thus says the Lord, the God of David your father: "I have heard your prayer, I have seen your tears; surely I will heal you. On the third day you shall go up to the house of the Lord. . . .""""

Then Isaiah said, "Take a lump of figs." So they took and laid it on the boil, and he recovered.

2 KINGS 20:5, 7

DANIEL

Prayer: Daniel prays

Now when Daniel knew that the writing was signed, he went home. And in his upper room, with his windows open toward Jerusalem, he knelt down on his knees three times that day, and prayed and gave thanks before his God, as was his custom since early days.

DANIEL 6:10

Answer

So the king gave the command, and they brought Daniel and cast him into the den of lions. But the king spoke, saying to Daniel, "Your God, whom you serve continually, He will deliver you." . . . Then Daniel said to the king, "O king, live forever! My God sent His angel and shut the lions' mouths, so that they have not hurt me, because I was found innocent before Him; and also, O king, I have done no wrong before you."

DANIEL 6:16, 21–22

Prayer: Daniel prays for revelation

Then I set my face toward the Lord God to make request by prayer and supplications, with fasting, sackcloth, and ashes. And I prayed to the LORD my God, and made confession, and said, "O Lord, great and awesome God, who keeps His covenant and mercy with those who love Him, and with those who keep His commandments."

DANIEL 9:3–4

Answer

Now while I was speaking, praying, and confessing my sin and the sin of my people Israel, and presenting my supplication before the LORD my God for the holy mountain of my God, yes, while I was speaking in prayer, the man Gabriel, whom I had seen in the vision at the beginning, being caused to fly swiftly, reached me about the time of the evening offering. And he informed me, and talked with me, and said, "O Daniel, I have now come forth to give you skill to understand."

DANIEL 9:20–22

JONAH

Prayer: Jonah prays

Then Jonah prayed to the LORD his God from the fish's belly . . .

"When my soul fainted within me,
I remembered the LORD;
And my prayer went up to You,
Into Your holy temple."

JONAH 2:1, 7

Answer

So the LORD spoke to the fish, and it vomited Jonah onto dry land.

JONAH 2:10

SIMEON

Prayer: Simeon waits for the Christ

And behold, there was a man in Jerusalem whose name was Simeon, and this man was just and devout, waiting for the Consolation of Israel, and the Holy Spirit was upon him. And it had been revealed to him by the Holy Spirit that he would not see death before he had seen the Lord's Christ.

LUKE 2:25–26

Answer

Lord, now You are letting Your servant depart in peace,

According to Your word;

For my eyes have seen Your salvation.

LUKE 2:29–30

PETER

Prayer: Restoration of Peter's mother-in-law

Now when Jesus had come into Peter's house, He saw his wife's mother lying sick with a fever.

MATTHEW 8:14

Answer

So He touched her hand, and the fever left her. And she arose and served them.

MATTHEW 8:15

WOMAN WITH THE ISSUE OF BLOOD

Prayer: Healing of issue of blood

For she said to herself, "If only I may touch His garment, I shall be made well."

MATTHEW 9:21

Answer

Jesus turned around, and when He saw her He said,

"Be of good cheer, daughter; your faith has made you well." And the woman was made well from that hour.

MATTHEW 9:22

JESUS

Prayer: Healing of blind men
When Jesus departed from there, two blind men followed Him, crying out and saying, "Son of David, have mercy on us!"

MATTHEW 9:27

Answer
Then He touched their eyes, saying, "According to your faith let it be to you."

MATTHEW 9:29

Prayer: The feeding of the five thousand
Then He commanded the multitudes to sit down on the grass. And He took the five loaves and the two fish, and looking up to heaven, He blessed and broke and gave the loaves to the disciples; and the disciples gave to the multitudes.

MATTHEW 14:19

Answer

So they all ate and were filled, and they took up twelve baskets full of the fragments that remained. Now those who had eaten were about five thousand men, besides women and children.

MATTHEW 14:20–21

Prayer: Healing of blind man

And behold, two blind men sitting by the road, when they heard that Jesus was passing by, cried out, saying, "Have mercy on us, O Lord, Son of David!"

MATTHEW 20:30

Answer

So Jesus had compassion and touched their eyes. And immediately their eyes received sight, and they followed Him.

MATTHEW 20:34

Prayer: Jesus prays for a submissive will

He went a little farther and fell on His face, and prayed, saying, "O My Father, if it is possible, let this cup pass from Me; nevertheless, not as I will, but as You will."

MATTHEW 26:39

Answer

Who, in the days of His flesh, when He had offered up prayers and supplications, with vehement cries and tears to Him who was able to save Him from death, and was heard because of His godly fear.

HEBREWS 5:7

Prayer: Healing of a paralytic

Then they came to Him, bringing a paralytic who was carried by four men. And when they could not come near Him because of the crowd, they uncovered the roof where He was. So when they had broken through, they let down the bed on which the paralytic was lying.

When Jesus saw their faith, He said to the paralytic, "Son, your sins are forgiven you."

MARK 2:3–5

Answer

Immediately he arose, took up the bed, and went out in the presence of them all, so that all were amazed and glorified God, saying, "We never saw anything like this!"

MARK 2:12

Prayer: Peter walks on the water

But when he saw that the wind was boisterous, he was afraid; and beginning to sink he cried out, saying, "Lord, save me!"

MATTHEW 14:30

Answer

And immediately Jesus stretched out His hand and caught him, and said to him, "O you of little faith, why did you doubt?" And when they got into the boat, the wind ceased.

MATTHEW 14:31–32

Prayer: Deliverance of Canaanite woman's daughter

Behold, a woman of Canaan came from that region and cried out to Him, saying, "Have mercy on me, O Lord, Son of David! My daughter is severely demon-possessed."

MATTHEW 15:22

Answer

Then Jesus answered and said to her, "O woman, great is your faith! Let it be to you as you desire." And her daughter was healed from that very hour.

MATTHEW 15:28

Prayer: Healing of epileptic son

"Lord, have mercy on my son, for he is an epileptic and suffers severely; for he often falls into the fire and often into the water."

MATTHEW 17:15

Answer

Jesus rebuked the demon, and it came out of him; and the child was cured from that very hour.

MATTHEW 17:18

Prayer: Healing of centurion's servant

"Therefore I did not even think myself worthy to come to You. But say the word, and my servant will be healed. For I also am a man placed under authority, having soldiers under me. And I say to one, 'Go,' and he goes; and to another, 'Come,' and he comes; and to my servant, 'Do this,' and he does it."

LUKE 7:7–8

Answer

When Jesus heard these things, He marveled at him,

and turned around and said to the crowd that followed Him, "I say to you, I have not found such great faith, not even in Israel!" And those who were sent, returning to the house, found the servant well who had been sick.

LUKE 7:9–10

Prayer: Cleansing of lepers

Then as He entered a certain village, there met Him ten men who were lepers, who stood afar off. And they lifted up their voices and said, "Jesus, Master, have mercy on us!"

LUKE 17:12–13

Answer

And one of them, when he saw that he was healed, returned, and with a loud voice glorified God.

LUKE 17:15

Prayer: Healing of nobleman's son

When he heard that Jesus had come out of Judea into Galilee, he went to Him and implored Him to come down and heal his son, for he was at the point of death.

JOHN 4:47

Answer

Then he inquired of them the hour when he got better. And they said to him, "Yesterday at the seventh hour the fever left him." So the father knew that it was at the same hour in which Jesus said to him, "Your son lives." And he himself believed, and his whole household.

JOHN 4:52–53

Prayer: Lazarus raised from the dead

Then they took away the stone from the place where the dead man was lying. And Jesus lifted up His eyes and said, "Father, I thank You that You have heard Me. And I know that You always hear Me, but because of the people who are standing by I said this, that they may believe that You sent Me." Now when He had said these things, He cried with a loud voice, "Lazarus, come forth!"

JOHN 11:41–43

Answer

He who had died came out bound hand and foot with graveclothes, and his face was wrapped with a cloth. Jesus said to them, "Loose him, and let him go."

JOHN 11:44

THIEF ON THE CROSS

Prayer: Of penitent thief

Then he said to Jesus, "Lord, remember me when You come into Your kingdom."

LUKE 23:42

Answer

Jesus said to him, "Assuredly, I say to you, today you will be with Me in Paradise."

LUKE 23:43

PETER

Prayer: The raising of Dorcas

Then Peter arose and went with them. When he had come, they brought him to the upper room. And all the widows stood by him weeping, showing the tunics and garments which Dorcas had made while she was with them.

ACTS 9:39

Answer

Then he gave her his hand and lifted her up; and

when he had called the saints and widows, he presented her alive.

ACTS 9:41

Prayer: Healing of lame man at Gate Beautiful

Peter said, "Silver and gold I do not have, but what I do have I give you: In the name of Jesus Christ of Nazareth, rise up and walk."

ACTS 3:6

Answer

So he, leaping up, stood and walked and entered the temple with them—walking, leaping, and praising God.

ACTS 3:8

Prayer: Peter released from prison

Peter was therefore kept in prison, but constant prayer was offered to God for him by the church.

ACTS 12:5

Answer

When Peter had come to himself, he said, "Now I know for certain that the Lord has sent His angel, and has delivered me from the hand of Herod and from all the expectation of the Jewish people."

ACTS 12:11

PAUL

Prayer: Paul prays for Publius's father
And it happened that the father of Publius lay sick of a fever and dysentery. Paul went in to him and prayed, and he laid his hands on him and healed him.

ACTS 28:8

Answer
So when this was done, the rest of those on the island who had diseases also came and were healed.

ACTS 28:9

Prayer: Paul and Silas released from jail
But at midnight Paul and Silas were praying and singing hymns to God, and the prisoners were listening to them.

ACTS 16:25

Answer

Suddenly there was a great earthquake, so that the foundations of the prison were shaken; and immediately all the doors were opened and everyone's chains were loosed.

ACTS 16:26

Prayer: The safety of the shipwrecked

"For there stood by me this night an angel of the God to whom I belong and whom I serve, saying, 'Do not be afraid, Paul; you must be brought before Caesar; and indeed God has granted you all those who sail with you.' Therefore take heart, men, for I believe God that it will be just as it was told me."

ACTS 27:23–25

Answer

And the rest, some on boards and some on parts of the ship. And so it was that they all escaped safely to land.

ACTS 27:44

INTERCESSORY PRAYER

Jesus is our Intercessor. He stands before our heavenly Father to represent us to Him. Jesus is our everything and in Him, God looks upon us and sees us as perfect. We can be assured that through Jesus Christ we belong to God and can rest in His presence. Therefore, the lives that we live should bring honor and glory to the heavenly Father, who gave His Son on the cross that we might have eternal life with our Lord.

JESUS' INTERCESSION FOR US

By so much more Jesus has become a surety of a better covenant. . . . Therefore He is also able to save to the uttermost those who come to God through Him, since He always lives to make intercession for them.

HEBREWS 7:22, 25

And the Lord said, "Simon, Simon! Indeed, Satan has asked for you, that he may sift you as wheat. But I have prayed for you, that your faith should not fail; and when you have returned to Me, strengthen your brethren."

LUKE 22:31–32

"In that day you will ask in My name, and I do not say to you that I shall pray the Father for you."

JOHN 16:26

"I pray for them. I do not pray for the world but for those whom You have given Me, for they are Yours. . . . I do not pray that You should take them out of the world, but that You should keep them from the evil one. . . . I do not pray for these alone, but also for those who will believe in Me through their word."

JOHN 17:9, 15, 20

Now He who searches the hearts knows what the mind of the Spirit is, because He makes intercession for the saints according to the will of God.

ROMANS 8:27

It is Christ who died, and furthermore is also risen, who is even at the right hand of God, who also makes intercession for us.

ROMANS 8:34

Now as He drew near, He saw the city and wept over it.

LUKE 19:41

Therefore, when Jesus saw her weeping, and the Jews who came with her weeping, He groaned in the spirit and was troubled. And He said, "Where have you laid him?"

They said to Him, "Lord, come and see."

Jesus wept. Then the Jews said, "See how He loved him!"

JOHN 11:33–36

Who, in the days of His flesh, when He had offered up prayers and supplications, with vehement cries and tears to Him who was able to save Him from death, and was heard because of His godly fear.

HEBREWS 5:7

OUR INTERCESSION FOR OTHERS

And the LORD said, "Because the outcry against Sodom and Gomorrah is great, and because their sin is very grave, I will go down now and see whether they have done altogether according to the outcry against it that has come to Me; and if not, I will know."

Then the men turned away from there and went toward Sodom, but Abraham still stood before the LORD. And Abraham came near and said, "Would You also destroy the righteous with the wicked? Suppose there were fifty righteous within the city; would You also destroy the place and not spare it for the fifty righteous that were in it? Far be it from You to do such a thing as this, to slay the righteous with the wicked, so that the righteous should be as the wicked; far be it from You! Shall not the Judge of all the earth do right?"

So the LORD said, "If I find in Sodom fifty righteous within the city, then I will spare all the place for their sakes."

Then Abraham answered and said, "Indeed now, I who am but dust and ashes have taken it upon myself to speak to the Lord: Suppose there were five less than the fifty righteous; would You destroy all of the city for lack of five?"

So He said, "If I find there forty-five, I will not destroy it."

And he spoke to Him yet again and said, "Suppose there should be forty found there?"

So He said, "I will not do it for the sake of forty."

Then he said, "Let not the Lord be angry, and I will speak: Suppose thirty should be found there?"

So He said, "I will not do it if I find thirty there."

And he said, "Indeed now, I have taken it upon myself to speak to the Lord: Suppose twenty should be found there?"

So He said, "I will not destroy it for the sake of twenty."

Then he said, "Let not the Lord be angry, and I will speak but once more: Suppose ten should be found there?"

And He said, "I will not destroy it for the sake of ten." So the LORD went His way as soon as He had finished speaking with Abraham; and Abraham returned to his place.

GENESIS 18:20–33

"And the Lord was very angry with Aaron and would have destroyed him; so I prayed for Aaron also at the same time. . . . Therefore I prayed to the LORD, and said: 'O Lord GOD, do not destroy Your people and Your inheritance whom You have redeemed through Your greatness, whom You have brought out of Egypt with a mighty hand.'"

DEUTERONOMY 9:20, 26

And Samuel said, "Gather all Israel to Mizpah, and I will pray to the LORD for you." . . . So the children of Israel said to Samuel, "Do not cease to cry out to the Lord our God for us, that He may save us from the hand of the Philistines."

1 SAMUEL 7:5, 8

"If My people who are called by My name will humble themselves, and pray and seek My face, and turn from their wicked ways, then I will hear from heaven, and will forgive their sin and heal their land."

2 CHRONICLES 7:14

He saw that there was no man,
And wondered that there was no intercessor;
Therefore His own arm brought salvation
    for Him;
And His own righteousness, it sustained Him.

ISAIAH 59:16

I have set watchmen on your walls, O
    Jerusalem;
They shall never hold their peace day or night.

You who make mention of the LORD, do not
keep silent.

ISAIAH 62:6

And there is no one who calls on Your name,
Who stirs himself up to take hold of You;
For You have hidden Your face from us,
And have consumed us because of our
iniquities.

ISAIAH 64:7

"Who has heard such a thing?
Who has seen such things?
Shall the earth be made to give birth in
one day?
Or shall a nation be born at once?
For as soon as Zion was in labor,
She gave birth to her children."

ISAIAH 66:8

And so it was, after the LORD had spoken these
words to Job, that the LORD said to Eliphaz the
Temanite, "My wrath is aroused against you and
your two friends, for you have not spoken of Me
what is right, as My servant Job has. Now therefore,

take for yourselves seven bulls and seven rams, go to My servant Job, and offer up for yourselves a burnt offering; and My servant Job shall pray for you. For I will accept him, lest I deal with you according to your folly; because you have not spoken of Me what is right, as My servant Job has."

So Eliphaz the Temanite and Bildad the Shuhite and Zophar the Naamathite went and did as the LORD commanded them; for the LORD had accepted Job. And the LORD restored Job's losses when he prayed for his friends. Indeed the LORD gave Job twice as much as he had before.

JOB 42:7–10

"So I sought for a man among them who would make a wall, and stand in the gap before Me on behalf of the land, that I should not destroy it; but I found no one."

EZEKIEL 22:30

Then I set my face toward the Lord God to make request by prayer and supplications, with fasting, sackcloth, and ashes. And I prayed to the LORD my God, and made confession, and said, "O Lord, great and awesome God, who keeps His covenant and mercy with those who love Him, and with those who keep His commandments."

DANIEL 9:3–4

"And shall God not avenge His own elect who cry out day and night to Him, though He bears long with them?"

LUKE 18:7

"I have surely seen the oppression of My people who are in Egypt; I have heard their groaning and have come down to deliver them. And now come, I will send you to Egypt."

ACTS 7:34

Brethren, my heart's desire and prayer to God for Israel is that they may be saved.

ROMANS 10:1

Now I beg you, brethren, through the Lord Jesus Christ, and through the love of the Spirit, that you strive together with me in prayers to God for me.

ROMANS 15:30

You also helping together in prayer for us, that thanks may be given by many persons on our behalf for the gift granted to us through many.

2 CORINTHIANS 1:11

Do not cease to give thanks for you, making mention of you in my prayers.

EPHESIANS 1:16

Praying always with all prayer and supplication in the Spirit, being watchful to this end with all perseverance and supplication for all the saints—and for me, that utterance may be given to me, that I may open my mouth boldly to make known the mystery of the gospel.

EPHESIANS 6:18–19

I thank my God upon every remembrance of you, always in every prayer of mine making request for you all with joy, for your fellowship in the gospel from the first day until now, being confident of this very thing, that He who has begun a good work in you will complete it until the day of Jesus Christ.

PHILIPPIANS 1:3–6

For this reason we also, since the day we heard it, do not cease to pray for you, and to ask that you may be filled with the knowledge of His will in all wisdom and spiritual understanding; that you may walk worthy of the Lord, fully pleasing Him, being fruitful in every good work and increasing in the knowledge of God; strengthened with all might, according to His glorious power, for all patience and longsuffering with joy; giving thanks to the Father who has qualified us to be partakers of the inheritance of the saints in the light. He has delivered us from the power of darkness and conveyed us into the kingdom of the Son of His love.

COLOSSIANS 1:9–13

For what thanks can we render to God for you, for all the joy with which we rejoice for your sake before our God, night and day praying exceedingly that we may see your face and perfect what is lacking in your faith?

Now may our God and Father Himself, and our Lord Jesus Christ, direct our way to you. And may the Lord make you increase and abound in love to one another and to all, just as we do to you, so that He may establish your hearts blameless in holiness

before our God and Father at the coming of our Lord
Jesus Christ with all His saints.

1 THESSALONIANS 3:9–13

Therefore we also pray always for you that our God
would count you worthy of this calling, and fulfill all
the good pleasure of His goodness and the work of
faith with power.

2 THESSALONIANS 1:11

Finally, brethren, pray for us, that the word of the
Lord may run swiftly and be glorified, just as it is with
you, and that we may be delivered from unreasonable
and wicked men; for not all have faith.

But the Lord is faithful, who will establish you
and guard you from the evil one. And we have confidence in the Lord concerning you, both that you do
and will do the things we command you.

Now may the Lord direct your hearts into the
love of God and into the patience of Christ.

2 THESSALONIANS 3:1–5

Therefore I exhort first of all that supplications,
prayers, intercessions, and giving of thanks be made
for all men, for kings and all who are in authority,

that we may lead a quiet and peaceable life in all god-liness and reverence.

1 TIMOTHY 2:1–2

But, meanwhile, also prepare a guest room for me, for I trust that through your prayers I shall be granted to you.

PHILEMON 22

Now this is the confidence that we have in Him, that if we ask anything according to His will, He hears us. And if we know that He hears us, whatever we ask, we know that we have the petitions that we have asked of Him.

If anyone sees his brother sinning a sin which does not lead to death, he will ask, and He will give him life for those who commit sin not leading to death. There is sin leading to death. I do not say that he should pray about that.

1 JOHN 5:14–16

Then his servants said to him, "What is this that you have done? You fasted and wept for the child while he was alive, but when the child died, you arose and ate food."

And he said, "While the child was alive, I fasted and wept; for I said, 'Who can tell whether the LORD will be gracious to me, that the child may live?'"

2 SAMUEL 12:21–22

"Return and tell Hezekiah the leader of My people, 'Thus says the LORD, the God of David your father: "I have heard your prayer, I have seen your tears; surely I will heal you. On the third day you shall go up to the house of the LORD."'"

2 KINGS 20:5

THE HOLY SPIRIT IN INTERCESSION

"If you then, being evil, know how to give good gifts to your children, how much more will your heavenly Father give the Holy Spirit to those who ask Him!"

LUKE 11:13

"Behold, I send the Promise of My Father upon you; but tarry in the city of Jerusalem until you are endued with power from on high."

LUKE 24:49

"But the Helper, the Holy Spirit, whom the Father will send in My name, He will teach you all things, and bring to your remembrance all things that I said to you."

JOHN 14:26

"But when the Helper comes, whom I shall send to you from the Father, the Spirit of truth who proceeds from the Father, He will testify of Me."

JOHN 15:26

When the Day of Pentecost had fully come, they were all with one accord in one place. And suddenly there came a sound from heaven, as of a rushing mighty wind, and it filled the whole house where they were sitting. Then there appeared to them divided tongues, as of fire, and one sat upon each of them. And they were all filled with the Holy Spirit and began to speak with other tongues, as the Spirit gave them utterance.

ACTS 2:1–4

For he who speaks in a tongue does not speak to men but to God, for no one understands him; however, in the spirit he speaks mysteries. But he who prophesies speaks edification and exhortation and comfort to men. He who speaks in a tongue edifies himself, but he who prophesies edifies the church. . . .

For if I pray in a tongue, my spirit prays, but my understanding is unfruitful. What is the conclusion then? I will pray with the spirit, and I will also pray with the understanding. I will sing with the spirit, and I will also sing with the understanding.

1 CORINTHIANS 14:2–4, 14–15

And being assembled together with them, He commanded them not to depart from Jerusalem, but to wait for the Promise of the Father, "which," He said, "you have heard from Me; for John truly baptized with water, but you shall be baptized with the Holy Spirit not many days from now."

ACTS 1:4–5

Likewise the Spirit also helps in our weaknesses. For we do not know what we should pray for as we ought, but the Spirit Himself makes intercession for us with groanings which cannot be uttered.

ROMANS 8:26

Praying always with all prayer and supplication in the Spirit, being watchful to this end with all perseverance and supplication for all the saints.

EPHESIANS 6:18

Continue earnestly in prayer, being vigilant in it with thanksgiving.

COLOSSIANS 4:2

But you, beloved, building yourselves up on your most holy faith, praying in the Holy Spirit, keep yourselves in the love of God, looking for the mercy of our Lord Jesus Christ unto eternal life.

JUDE 1:20–21

"However, when He, the Spirit of truth, has come, He will guide you into all truth; for He will not speak on His own authority, but whatever He hears He will speak; and He will tell you things to come."

JOHN 16:13

Then they laid hands on them, and they received the Holy Spirit.

ACTS 8:17

And when Paul had laid hands on them, the Holy Spirit came upon them, and they spoke with tongues and prophesied.

ACTS 19:6

GREAT INTERCESSORS

The Bible is filled with great intercessors who have pleaded their case for their brothers and sisters before God. In this section I have chosen nineteen such men and women of God. It's obvious that we are called to pray for one another and seek God's guidance for our fellow Christians. When we lift someone up in prayer, we are doing what God has called us to do. Paul prayed in 1 Thessalonians 5:23, "Now may the God of peace Himself sanctify you completely; and may your whole spirit, soul, and body be preserved blameless at the coming of our Lord Jesus Christ." We should follow Paul's lead and pray diligently for our fellow Christians.

JESUS CHRIST

And behold, there was a man in Jerusalem whose name was Simeon, and this man was just and devout, waiting for the Consolation of Israel, and the Holy Spirit was upon him. And it had been revealed to him by the Holy Spirit that he would not see death before he had seen the Lord's Christ. So he came by the Spirit into the temple. And when the parents brought in the Child Jesus, to do for Him according to the custom of the law, he took Him up in his arms and blessed God and said:

> "Lord, now You are letting Your servant depart
> in peace,
> According to Your word;
> For my eyes have seen Your salvation . . . "

Then Simeon blessed them, and said to Mary His mother, "Behold, this Child is destined for the fall and rising of many in Israel, and for a sign which will be spoken against."

LUKE 2:25–30, 34

Dedication

When all the people were baptized, it came to pass that Jesus also was baptized; and while He prayed, the heaven was opened. And the Holy Spirit descended in bodily form like a dove upon Him, and a voice came from heaven which said, "You are My beloved Son; in You I am well pleased."

LUKE 3:21–22

Separation

However, the report went around concerning Him all the more; and great multitudes came together to hear, and to be healed by Him of their infirmities. So He Himself often withdrew into the wilderness and prayed.

LUKE 5:15–16

Direction

Now it came to pass in those days that He went out to the mountain to pray, and continued all night in prayer to God. And when it was day, He called His disciples to Himself; and from them He chose twelve whom He also named apostles: Simon, whom He also named Peter, and Andrew his brother; James and John; Philip and Bartholomew; Matthew and Thomas; James the son of Alphaeus, and Simon called the Zealot; Judas the son of James, and Judas Iscariot who also became a traitor.

LUKE 6:12–16

Revelation

And it happened, as He was alone praying, that His disciples joined Him, and He asked them, saying, "Who do the crowds say that I am?"

So they answered and said, "John the Baptist, but some say Elijah; and others say that one of the old prophets has risen again."

He said to them, "But who do you say that I am?"

Peter answered and said, "The Christ of God."

LUKE 9:18–20

Glorification

As He prayed, the appearance of His face was altered, and His robe became white and glistening.

LUKE 9:29

Jesus spoke these words, lifted up His eyes to heaven, and said: "Father, the hour has come. Glorify Your Son, that Your Son also may glorify You, as You have given Him authority over all flesh, that He should give eternal life to as many as You have given Him. And this is eternal life, that they may know You, the only true God, and Jesus Christ whom You have sent. I have glorified You on the earth. I have finished the work which You have given Me to do. And now, O Father, glorify Me together with Yourself, with the glory which I had with You before the world was.

"I have manifested Your name to the men whom You have given Me out of the world. They were Yours,

You gave them to Me, and they have kept Your word. Now they have known that all things which You have given Me are from You. For I have given to them the words which You have given Me; and they have received them, and have known surely that I came forth from You; and they have believed that You sent Me.

"I pray for them. I do not pray for the world but for those whom You have given Me, for they are Yours. And all Mine are Yours, and Yours are Mine, and I am glorified in them."

JOHN 17:1–10

Obedience

Coming out, He went to the Mount of Olives, as He was accustomed, and His disciples also followed Him. When He came to the place, He said to them, "Pray that you may not enter into temptation."

And He was withdrawn from them about a stone's throw, and He knelt down and prayed, saying, "Father, if it is Your will, take this cup away from Me; nevertheless not My will, but Yours, be done." Then an angel appeared to Him from heaven, strengthening Him. And being in agony, He prayed more earnestly. Then His sweat became like great drops of blood falling down to the ground.

When He rose up from prayer, and had come to His disciples, He found them sleeping from sorrow. Then He said to them, "Why do you sleep? Rise and pray, lest you enter into temptation."

LUKE 22:39–46

Redemption

"The Redeemer will come to Zion,
>   And to those who turn from transgression in
>   Jacob,"
Says the LORD.

"As for Me," says the LORD, "this is My covenant with them: My Spirit who is upon you, and My words which I have put in your mouth, shall not depart from your mouth, nor from the mouth of your descendants, nor from the mouth of your descendants' descendants," says the LORD, "from this time and forevermore."

ISAIAH 59:20–21

Persecutors

But the chief priests and elders persuaded the multitudes that they should ask for Barabbas and destroy

Jesus. The governor answered and said to them, "Which of the two do you want me to release to you?"

They said, "Barabbas!"

Pilate said to them, "What then shall I do with Jesus who is called Christ?"

They all said to him, "Let Him be crucified!" . . .

And they stripped Him and put a scarlet robe on Him. When they had twisted a crown of thorns, they put it on His head, and a reed in His right hand. And they bowed the knee before Him and mocked Him, saying, "Hail, King of the Jews!" Then they spat on Him, and took the reed and struck Him on the head. And when they had mocked Him, they took the robe off Him, put His own clothes on Him, and led Him away to be crucified.

MATTHEW 27:20−22, 28−31

Prophecy

My God, My God, why have You forsaken Me?
Why are You so far from helping Me,
And from the words of My groaning? . . .

I am poured out like water,
And all My bones are out of joint;
My heart is like wax;

It has melted within Me.
My strength is dried up like a potsherd,
And My tongue clings to My jaws;
You have brought Me to the dust of death.

For dogs have surrounded Me;
The congregation of the wicked has
enclosed Me.
They pierced My hands and My feet;
I can count all My bones.
They look and stare at Me.
They divide My garments among them,
And for My clothing they cast lots.

PSALM 22:1, 14–18

Presentation

And when Jesus had cried out with a loud voice, He said, "Father, 'into Your hands I commit My spirit.'" Having said this, He breathed His last.

LUKE 23:46

But Christ came as High Priest of the good things to come, with the greater and more perfect tabernacle not made with hands, that is, not of this creation. Not with the blood of goats and calves, but with His own blood He entered the Most Holy Place once for all, having obtained eternal redemption. . . . And for this reason He is the Mediator of the new covenant, by means of death, for the redemption of the transgressions under the first covenant, that those who are called may receive the promise of the eternal inheritance.

HEBREWS 9:11–12, 15

PAUL

Behold, He Prayeth
So the Lord said to him, "Arise and go to the street called Straight, and inquire at the house of Judas for one called Saul of Tarsus, for behold, he is praying."

ACTS 9:11

Power and Knowledge
Therefore I also, after I heard of your faith in the Lord Jesus and your love for all the saints, do not cease to give thanks for you, making mention of you in my prayers: that the God of our Lord Jesus Christ, the Father of glory, may give to you the spirit of wisdom and revelation in the knowledge of Him, the eyes of your understanding being enlightened; that you may

know what is the hope of His calling, what are the riches of the glory of His inheritance in the saints, and what is the exceeding greatness of His power toward us who believe, according to the working of His mighty power which He worked in Christ when He raised Him from the dead and seated Him at His right hand in the heavenly places, far above all principality and power and might and dominion, and every name that is named, not only in this age but also in that which is to come.

EPHESIANS 1:15–21

Personal Pentecost

Therefore I ask that you do not lose heart at my tribulations for you, which is your glory.

For this reason I bow my knees to the Father of our Lord Jesus Christ, from whom the whole family in heaven and earth is named, that He would grant you, according to the riches of His glory, to be strengthened with might through His Spirit in the inner man, that Christ may dwell in your hearts through faith; that you, being rooted and grounded in love, may be able to comprehend with all the saints what is the width and length and depth and height—to know the love of Christ which passes knowledge; that you may be filled with all the fullness of God.

Now to Him who is able to do exceedingly abundantly above all that we ask or think, according to the power that works in us, to Him be glory in the church by Christ Jesus to all generations, forever and ever. Amen.

EPHESIANS 3:13–21

Perseverance

And this I pray, that your love may abound still more and more in knowledge and all discernment, that you may approve the things that are excellent, that you may be sincere and without offense till the day of Christ, being filled with the fruits of righteousness which are by Jesus Christ, to the glory and praise of God.

PHILIPPIANS 1:9–11

Perception

For this reason we also, since the day we heard it, do not cease to pray for you, and to ask that you may be filled with the knowledge of His will in all wisdom and spiritual understanding; that you may walk worthy of the Lord, fully pleasing Him, being fruitful in every good work and increasing in the knowledge of God; strengthened with all might, according to His glorious power, for all patience and longsuffering with joy; giving thanks to the Father who has qualified us to be partakers of the inheritance of the saints in the light. He has delivered us from the power of darkness and conveyed us into the kingdom of the Son of His love.

COLOSSIANS 1:9–13

Perfection

For what thanks can we render to God for you, for all the joy with which we rejoice for your sake before our God, night and day praying exceedingly that we may see your face and perfect what is lacking in your faith?

Now may our God and Father Himself, and our Lord Jesus Christ, direct our way to you. And may the Lord make you increase and abound in love to one another and to all, just as we do to you, so that He may establish your hearts blameless in holiness before our God and Father at the coming of our Lord Jesus Christ with all His saints.

1 THESSALONIANS 3:9–13

Pain

And lest I should be exalted above measure by the abundance of the revelations, a thorn in the flesh was given to me, a messenger of Satan to buffet me, lest I be exalted above measure. Concerning this thing I pleaded with the Lord three times that it might depart from me. And He said to me, "My grace is sufficient for you, for My strength is made perfect in weakness." Therefore most gladly I will rather boast in my infirmities, that the power of Christ may rest upon me.

2 CORINTHIANS 12:7–9

Pressures

Finally, brethren, pray for us, that the word of the Lord may run swiftly and be glorified, just as it is with you, and that we may be delivered from unreasonable and wicked men; for not all have faith.

2 THESSALONIANS 3:1–2

Peace

Now may the Lord of peace Himself give you peace always in every way. The Lord be with you all.

2 THESSALONIANS 3:16

Pleasing Life

Now may the God of peace who brought up our Lord
Jesus from the dead, that great Shepherd of the sheep,
through the blood of the everlasting covenant, make
you complete in every good work to do His will, working in you what is well pleasing in His sight, through
Jesus Christ, to whom be glory forever and ever.
Amen.

HEBREWS 13:20–21

Preserved

Now may the God of peace Himself sanctify you
completely; and may your whole spirit, soul, and
body be preserved blameless at the coming of our
Lord Jesus Christ.

1 THESSALONIANS 5:23

Pleasure

Therefore we also pray always for you that our God
would count you worthy of this calling, and fulfill
all the good pleasure of His goodness and the work
of faith with power, that the name of our Lord Jesus
Christ may be glorified in you, and you in Him,

according to the grace of our God and the Lord Jesus
Christ.

2 THESSALONIANS 1:11–12

Permanency

Pray without ceasing, in everything give thanks; for
this is the will of God in Christ Jesus for you. . . .

Now may the God of peace Himself sanctify you
completely; and may your whole spirit, soul, and body
be preserved blameless at the coming of our Lord
Jesus Christ. He who calls you is faithful, who also
will do it.

Brethren, pray for us.

1 THESSALONIANS 5:17–18, 23–25

JEHOSHAPHAT

So the king of Israel and Jehoshaphat the king of
Judah went up to Ramoth Gilead. And the king of
Israel said to Jehoshaphat, "I will disguise myself and
go into battle; but you put on your robes." So the king
of Israel disguised himself, and they went into battle.

Now the king of Syria had commanded the
captains of the chariots who were with him, saying,

"Fight with no one small or great, but only with the king of Israel."

So it was, when the captains of the chariots saw Jehoshaphat, that they said, "It is the king of Israel!" Therefore they surrounded him to attack; but Jehoshaphat cried out, and the LORD helped him, and God diverted them from him.

2 CHRONICLES 18:28–31

Then Jehoshaphat stood in the assembly of Judah and Jerusalem, in the house of the LORD, before the new court, and said: "O LORD God of our fathers, are You not God in heaven, and do You not rule over all the kingdoms of the nations, and in Your hand is there not power and might, so that no one is able to withstand You? Are You not our God, who drove out the inhabitants of this land before Your people Israel, and gave it to the descendants of Abraham Your friend forever? And they dwell in it, and have built You a sanctuary in it for Your name, saying, 'If disaster comes upon us—sword, judgment, pestilence, or famine—we will stand before this temple and in Your presence (for Your name is in this temple), and cry out to You in our affliction, and You will hear and save.'"

2 CHRONICLES 20:5–9

EZRA

Then I proclaimed a fast there at the river of Ahava, that we might humble ourselves before our God, to seek from Him the right way for us and our little ones and all our possessions. For I was ashamed to request of the king an escort of soldiers and horsemen to help us against the enemy on the road, because we had spoken to the king, saying, "The hand of our God is upon all those for good who seek Him, but His power and His wrath are against all those who forsake Him." So we fasted and entreated our God for this, and He answered our prayer.

EZRA 8:21–23

ZACHARIAS

And the whole multitude of the people was praying outside at the hour of incense. Then an angel of the Lord appeared to him, standing on the right side of the altar of incense. And when Zacharias saw him, he was troubled, and fear fell upon him.

But the angel said to him, "Do not be afraid, Zacharias, for your prayer is heard; and your wife

Elizabeth will bear you a son, and you shall call his name John."

LUKE 1:10–13

HEZEKIAH

"Go and tell Hezekiah, 'Thus says the LORD, the God of David your father: "I have heard your prayer, I have seen your tears; surely I will add to your days fifteen years. I will deliver you and this city from the hand of the king of Assyria, and I will defend this city."' And this is the sign to you from the LORD, that the LORD will do this thing which He has spoken: Behold, I will bring the shadow on the sundial, which has gone down with the sun on the sundial of Ahaz, ten degrees backward." So the sun returned ten degrees on the dial by which it had gone down.

This is the writing of Hezekiah king of Judah, when he had been sick and had recovered from his sickness.

ISAIAH 38:5–9

JEREMIAH

"Blessed is the man who trusts in the LORD,
    And whose hope is the LORD.

For he shall be like a tree planted by the waters,
Which spreads out its roots by the river,
And will not fear when heat comes;
But its leaf will be green,
And will not be anxious in the year of drought,
Nor will cease from yielding fruit.

"The heart is deceitful above all things,
And desperately wicked;
Who can know it?
I, the LORD, search the heart,
I test the mind,
Even to give every man according to his ways,
According to the fruit of his doings.

"As a partridge that broods but does not hatch,
So is he who gets riches, but not by right;
It will leave him in the midst of his days,
And at his end he will be a fool."

A glorious high throne from the beginning
Is the place of our sanctuary.
O LORD, the hope of Israel,
All who forsake You shall be ashamed.

"Those who depart from Me
Shall be written in the earth,
Because they have forsaken the Lord,
The fountain of living waters."

Heal me, O Lord, and I shall be healed;
Save me, and I shall be saved,
For You are my praise.
Indeed they say to me,
"Where is the word of the Lord?
Let it come now!"
As for me, I have not hurried away from being a
        shepherd who follows You,
Nor have I desired the woeful day;
You know what came out of my lips;
It was right there before You.
Do not be a terror to me;
You are my hope in the day of doom.
Let them be ashamed who persecute me,
But do not let me be put to shame;
Let them be dismayed,
But do not let me be dismayed.
Bring on them the day of doom,
And destroy them with double destruction!

JEREMIAH 17:7–18

MOSES

"Therefore I prayed to the Lord, and said: 'O Lord God, do not destroy Your people and Your inheritance whom You have redeemed through Your greatness, whom You have brought out of Egypt with a mighty hand. Remember Your servants, Abraham, Isaac, and Jacob; do not look on the stubbornness of this people, or on their wickedness or their sin, lest the land from which You brought us should say, "Because the Lord was not able to bring them to the land which He promised them, and because He hated them, He has brought them out to kill them in the wilderness." Yet they are Your people and Your inheritance, whom You brought out by Your mighty power and by Your outstretched arm.'"

DEUTERONOMY 9:26–29

JACOB

"Deliver me, I pray, from the hand of my brother, from the hand of Esau; for I fear him, lest he come and attack me and the mother with the children. For You said, 'I will surely treat you well, and make your descendants as the sand of the sea, which cannot be numbered for multitude.'"

So he lodged there that same night, and took what came to his hand as a present for Esau his brother: two hundred female goats and twenty male goats, two hundred ewes and twenty rams, thirty milk camels with their colts, forty cows and ten bulls, twenty female donkeys and ten foals. Then he delivered them to the hand of his servants, every drove by itself, and said to his servants, "Pass over before me, and put some distance between successive droves." And he commanded the first one, saying, "When Esau my brother meets you and asks you, saying, 'To whom do you belong, and where are you going? Whose are these in front of you?' then you shall say, 'They are your servant Jacob's. It is a present sent to my lord Esau; and behold, he also is behind us.'"

GENESIS 32:11–18

MARY

And Mary said:

"My soul magnifies the Lord,
And my spirit has rejoiced in God my Savior.

For He has regarded the lowly state of His
      maidservant;
For behold, henceforth all generations will call
      me blessed.
For He who is mighty has done great things
      for me,
And holy is His name.
And His mercy is on those who fear Him
From generation to generation.
He has shown strength with His arm;
He has scattered the proud in the imagination
      of their hearts.
He has put down the mighty from their thrones,
And exalted the lowly.
He has filled the hungry with good things,
And the rich He has sent away empty.
He has helped His servant Israel,
In remembrance of His mercy,
As He spoke to our fathers,
To Abraham and to his seed forever."

LUKE 1:46–55

DANIEL

Now on the twenty-fourth day of the first month, as I was by the side of the great river, that is, the Tigris, I lifted my eyes and looked, and behold, a certain man clothed in linen, whose waist was girded with gold of Uphaz! His body was like beryl, his face like the appearance of lightning, his eyes like torches of fire, his arms and feet like burnished bronze in color, and the sound of his words like the voice of a multitude.

And I, Daniel, alone saw the vision, for the men who were with me did not see the vision; but a great terror fell upon them, so that they fled to hide themselves. Therefore I was left alone when I saw this great vision, and no strength remained in me; for my vigor was turned to frailty in me, and I retained no strength. Yet I heard the sound of his words; and while I heard the sound of his words I was in a deep sleep on my face, with my face to the ground.

Suddenly, a hand touched me, which made me tremble on my knees and on the palms of my hands. And he said to me, "O Daniel, man greatly beloved, understand the words that I speak to you, and stand upright, for I have now been sent to you." While he was speaking this word to me, I stood trembling.

Then he said to me, "Do not fear, Daniel, for from the first day that you set your heart to understand, and to humble yourself before your God, your words were heard; and I have come because of your words. But the prince of the kingdom of Persia withstood me twenty-one days; and behold, Michael, one of the chief princes, came to help me, for I had been left alone there with the kings of Persia. Now I have come to make you understand what will happen to your people in the latter days, for the vision refers to many days yet to come." . . .

Then he said, "Do you know why I have come to you? And now I must return to fight with the prince of Persia; and when I have gone forth, indeed the prince of Greece will come. But I will tell you what is noted in the Scripture of Truth. (No one upholds me against these, except Michael your prince."

DANIEL 10:4–14, 20–21

CORNELIUS

And they said, "Cornelius the centurion, a just man, one who fears God and has a good reputation among all the nation of the Jews, was divinely instructed by a holy angel to summon you to his house, and to hear words from you." . . .

And the following day they entered Caesarea. Now Cornelius was waiting for them, and had called together his relatives and close friends. . . .

"Therefore I came without objection as soon as I was sent for. I ask, then, for what reason have you sent for me?"

So Cornelius said, "Four days ago I was fasting until this hour; and at the ninth hour I prayed in my house, and behold, a man stood before me in bright clothing, and said, 'Cornelius, your prayer has been heard, and your alms are remembered in the sight of God.'"

ACTS 10:22, 24, 29–31

ABRAHAM

And Abraham came near and said, "Would You also destroy the righteous with the wicked? Suppose there were fifty righteous within the city; would You also destroy the place and not spare it for the fifty righteous that were in it? Far be it from You to do such a thing as this, to slay the righteous with the wicked, so that the righteous should be as the wicked; far be it from You! Shall not the Judge of all the earth do right?"

So the LORD said, "If I find in Sodom fifty righteous within the city, then I will spare all the place for their sakes."

Then Abraham answered and said, "Indeed now, I who am but dust and ashes have taken it upon myself to speak to the Lord: Suppose there were five less than the fifty righteous; would You destroy all of the city for lack of five?"

So He said, "If I find there forty-five, I will not destroy it."

And he spoke to Him yet again and said, "Suppose there should be forty found there?"

So He said, "I will not do it for the sake of forty."

Then he said, "Let not the Lord be angry, and I will speak: Suppose thirty should be found there?"

So He said, "I will not do it if I find thirty there."

And he said, "Indeed now, I have taken it upon myself to speak to the Lord: Suppose twenty should be found there?"

So He said, "I will not destroy it for the sake of twenty."

Then he said, "Let not the Lord be angry, and

I will speak but once more: Suppose ten should be found there?"

And He said, "I will not destroy it for the sake of ten." So the LORD went His way as soon as He had finished speaking with Abraham; and Abraham returned to his place.

GENESIS 18:23–33

HOSEA

Yes, he struggled with the Angel and prevailed;
 He wept, and sought favor from Him.
 He found Him in Bethel,
 And there He spoke to us—
 That is, the LORD God of hosts.
 The LORD is His memorable name.
 So you, by the help of your God, return;
 Observe mercy and justice,
 And wait on your God continually.

HOSEA 12:4–6

ISAAC

Now Isaac pleaded with the LORD for his wife, because she was barren; and the LORD granted his plea, and Rebekah his wife conceived.

GENESIS 25:21

JOB

And the LORD restored Job's losses when he prayed for his friends. Indeed the LORD gave Job twice as much as he had before.

JOB 42:10

MANASSEH

Now when he was in affliction, he implored the LORD his God, and humbled himself greatly before the God of his fathers, and prayed to Him; and He received his entreaty, heard his supplication, and brought him back to Jerusalem into his kingdom. Then Manasseh knew that the LORD was God.

2 CHRONICLES 33:12–13

HANNAH

And she said, "O my lord! As your soul lives, my lord, I am the woman who stood by you here, praying to the LORD. For this child I prayed, and the LORD has granted me my petition which I asked of Him. Therefore I also have lent him to the LORD; as long as he lives he shall be lent to the LORD." So they worshiped the LORD there.

1 SAMUEL 1:26–28

And Hannah prayed and said:

"My heart rejoices in the LORD;
My horn is exalted in the LORD.
I smile at my enemies,
Because I rejoice in Your salvation.

"No one is holy like the LORD,
For there is none besides You,
Nor is there any rock like our God.

"Talk no more so very proudly;
Let no arrogance come from your mouth,

For the LORD is the God of knowledge;
And by Him actions are weighed."

1 SAMUEL 2:1–3

NEHEMIAH

The words of Nehemiah the son of Hachaliah. . . .

And they said to me, "The survivors who are left from the captivity in the province are there in great distress and reproach. The wall of Jerusalem is also broken down, and its gates are burned with fire."

So it was, when I heard these words, that I sat down and wept, and mourned for many days; I was fasting and praying before the God of heaven.

And I said: "I pray, LORD God of heaven, O great and awesome God, You who keep Your covenant and mercy with those who love You and observe Your commandments, please let Your ear be attentive and Your eyes open, that You may hear the prayer of Your servant which I pray before You now, day and night, for the children of Israel Your servants, and confess the sins of the children of Israel which we have sinned against You. Both my father's house and I have sinned. We have acted very corruptly against You, and have not kept the commandments, the statutes, nor the ordinances which You commanded Your servant Moses. Remember, I pray, the word that You commanded Your servant Moses, saying, 'If you are unfaithful, I will scatter you among the nations; but if you return to Me, and keep My commandments and do them, though some of you were cast out to the farthest part of the heavens, yet I will gather them from there, and bring them to the place which I have chosen as a dwelling for My name.' Now these are Your servants and Your people, whom You have redeemed by Your great power, and by Your strong hand. O Lord, I pray, please let Your ear be attentive to the prayer of Your servant, and to the prayer of Your servants who desire to fear Your name; and let Your servant prosper this day, I pray, and grant him mercy in the sight of this man."

For I was the king's cupbearer.

NEHEMIAH 1:1, 3–11

PRAYER PROMISES

The Bible is filled with prayer promises for our fellow Christians. Spiritual and physical healing, prosperity, revival, and guidance—we are called to be prayer partners in all of these occasions. Jeremiah 29:13 says, "You will seek Me and find Me, when you search for Me with all your heart." Prayer is given by the Lord as a two-way communication with Him. Therefore let us come boldly to the throne of grace and ask the Father to bless us with answers and guide us as we seek to serve Him faithfully in prayer.

PRAYER FOR OTHERS

And for me, that utterance may be given to me, that I may open my mouth boldly to make known the mystery of the gospel, for which I am an ambassador in chains; that in it I may speak boldly, as I ought to speak.

EPHESIANS 6:19–20

Brethren, pray for us.

1 THESSALONIANS 5:25

Finally, brethren, pray for us, that the word of the Lord may run swiftly and be glorified, just as it is with you.

2 THESSALONIANS 3:1

Hold fast the pattern of sound words which you have heard from me, in faith and love which are in Christ Jesus. That good thing which was committed to you, keep by the Holy Spirit who dwells in us.

2 TIMOTHY 1:13–14

"For the eyes of the LORD are on the righteous,
And His ears are open to their prayers;
But the face of the LORD is against those who
        do evil."

1 PETER 3:12

When my soul fainted within me,
I remembered the LORD;
And my prayer went up to You,
Into Your holy temple.

JONAH 2:7

Then Jesus went into the temple of God and drove out all those who bought and sold in the temple, and overturned the tables of the money changers and the seats of those who sold doves. And He said to them, "It is written, 'My house shall be called a house of prayer,' but you have made it a 'den of thieves.'"

MATTHEW 21:12–13

For this reason we also, since the day we heard it, do not cease to pray for you, and to ask that you may be filled with the knowledge of His will in all wisdom and spiritual understanding; that you may walk worthy of the Lord, fully pleasing Him, being fruitful in every good work and increasing in the knowledge of God; strengthened with all might, according to His glorious power, for all patience and longsuffering with joy; giving thanks to the Father who has qualified us to be partakers of the inheritance of the saints in the light. He has delivered us from the power of darkness and conveyed us into the kingdom of the Son of His love, in whom we have redemption through His blood, the forgiveness of sins.

COLOSSIANS 1:9–14

These all continued with one accord in prayer and supplication, with the women and Mary the mother of Jesus, and with His brothers. . . .

And they prayed and said, "You, O Lord, who know the hearts of all, show which of these two You have chosen." . . .

And they cast their lots, and the lot fell on Matthias. And he was numbered with the eleven apostles.

ACTS 1:14, 24, 26

And when they had prayed, the place where they were assembled together was shaken; and they were all filled with the Holy Spirit, and they spoke the word of God with boldness.

ACTS 4:31

A devout man and one who feared God with all his household, who gave alms generously to the people, and prayed to God always. . . .

The next day, as they went on their journey and drew near the city, Peter went up on the housetop to pray, about the sixth hour. . . .

So Cornelius said, "Four days ago I was fasting

until this hour; and at the ninth hour I prayed in my house, and behold, a man stood before me in bright clothing, and said, 'Cornelius, your prayer has been heard, and your alms are remembered in the sight of God.'"

ACTS 10:2, 9, 30–31

Peter was therefore kept in prison, but constant prayer was offered to God for him by the church.

ACTS 12:5

Then, having fasted and prayed, and laid hands on them, they sent them away.

ACTS 13:3

So when they had appointed elders in every church, and prayed with fasting, they commended them to the Lord in whom they had believed.

ACTS 14:23

"But we will give ourselves continually to prayer and to the ministry of the word."

ACTS 6:4

Now there was a certain disciple at Damascus named Ananias; and to him the Lord said in a vision, "Ananias."

And he said, "Here I am, Lord."

So the Lord said to him, "Arise and go to the street called Straight, and inquire at the house of Judas for one called Saul of Tarsus, for behold, he is praying. And in a vision he has seen a man named Ananias coming in and putting his hand on him, so that he might receive his sight."

Then Ananias answered, "Lord, I have heard from many about this man, how much harm he has done to Your saints in Jerusalem. And here he has authority from the chief priests to bind all who call on Your name."

But the Lord said to him, "Go, for he is a chosen vessel of Mine to bear My name before Gentiles, kings, and the children of Israel."

ACTS 9:10–15

Therefore the LORD brought upon them the captains of the army of the king of Assyria, who took Manasseh with hooks, bound him with bronze fetters, and carried him off to Babylon.... [Manasseh] prayed to Him; and He received his entreaty, heard his supplication, and brought him back to Jerusalem into his kingdom. Then Manasseh knew that the LORD was God.

2 CHRONICLES 33:11, 13

Show us Your mercy, LORD,
And grant us Your salvation.

PSALM 85:7

Behold, the LORD's hand is not shortened,
That it cannot save;
Nor His ear heavy,
That it cannot hear.

ISAIAH 59:1

"And you will seek Me and find Me, when you search for Me with all your heart."

JEREMIAH 29:13

And He said to him, "Arise, go your way. Your faith has made you well."

LUKE 17:19

But at midnight Paul and Silas were praying and singing hymns to God, and the prisoners were listening to them. Suddenly there was a great earthquake, so that the foundations of the prison were shaken; and immediately all the doors were opened and everyone's chains were loosed. And the keeper of the prison, awaking from sleep and seeing the prison doors open, supposing the prisoners had fled, drew his sword and was about to kill himself. But Paul called with a loud voice, saying, "Do yourself no harm, for we are all here."

Then he called for a light, ran in, and fell down trembling before Paul and Silas. And he brought them out and said, "Sirs, what must I do to be saved?"

So they said, "Believe on the Lord Jesus Christ, and you will be saved, you and your household." Then they spoke the word of the Lord to him and to all who were in his house. And he took them the same hour of the night and washed their stripes. And immediately he and all his family were baptized. Now when he had brought them into his house, he set food before them; and he rejoiced, having believed in God with all his household.

And when it was day, the magistrates sent the officers, saying, "Let those men go."

ACTS 16:25–35

"For what great nation is there that has God so near to it, as the LORD our God is to us, for whatever reason we may call upon Him? . . . especially concerning the day you stood before the LORD your God in Horeb, when the LORD said to me, 'Gather the people to Me, and I will let them hear My words, that they may learn to fear Me all the days they live on the earth, and that they may teach their children.'"

DEUTERONOMY 4:7, 10

And Samuel said, "Gather all Israel to Mizpah, and I will pray to the LORD for you." So they gathered together at Mizpah, drew water, and poured it out before the LORD. And they fasted that day, and said there, "We have sinned against the LORD." And Samuel judged the children of Israel at Mizpah. . . .

And Samuel took a suckling lamb and offered it as a whole burnt offering to the LORD. Then Samuel cried out to the LORD for Israel, and the LORD answered him.

1 SAMUEL 7:5–6, 9

"That Your eyes may be open toward this temple night and day, toward the place of which You said, 'My name shall be there,' that You may hear the prayer which Your servant makes toward this place." . . .

"When there is famine in the land, pestilence or blight or mildew, locusts or grasshoppers; when their enemy besieges them in the land of their cities; whatever plague or whatever sickness there is; whatever prayer, whatever supplication is made by anyone, or by all Your people Israel, when each one knows the plague of his own heart, and spreads out his hands toward this temple: then hear in heaven Your dwelling place, and forgive, and act, and give to everyone according to all his ways, whose heart You know (for You alone know the hearts of all the sons of men)."

1 KINGS 8:29, 37–39

"Yet when they come to themselves in the land where they were carried captive, and repent, and make supplication to You in the land of those who took them captive, saying, 'We have sinned and done wrong, we have committed wickedness'; and when they return to You with all their heart and with all their soul in the land of their enemies who led them away captive, and pray to You toward their land which You gave to their fathers, the city which You have chosen and the temple which I have built for Your name: then hear in heaven Your dwelling place their prayer and their supplication, and maintain their cause, and forgive

Your people who have sinned against You, and all their transgressions which they have transgressed against You; and grant them compassion before those who took them captive, that they may have compassion on them (for they are Your people and Your inheritance, whom You brought out of Egypt, out of the iron furnace), that Your eyes may be open to the supplication of Your servant and the supplication of Your people Israel, to listen to them whenever they call to You. For You separated them from among all the peoples of the earth to be Your inheritance, as You spoke by Your servant Moses, when You brought our fathers out of Egypt, O Lord GOD."

And so it was, when Solomon had finished praying all this prayer and supplication to the LORD, that he arose from before the altar of the LORD, from kneeling on his knees with his hands spread up to heaven. Then he stood and blessed all the assembly of Israel with a loud voice, saying: "Blessed be the LORD, who has given rest to His people Israel, according to all that He promised. There has not failed one word of all His good promise, which He promised through His servant Moses. May the LORD our God be with us, as He was with our fathers. May He not leave us nor forsake us, that He may incline our hearts to Himself, to walk in all His ways, and to keep His commandments and His statutes and His judgments, which He commanded our fathers. And may these words of mine, with which I have made supplication before the LORD, be near the LORD our God day and night, that He may maintain the cause of His servant and the cause of His people Israel, as each day may require."

1 KINGS 8:47–59

And Asa cried out to the LORD his God, and said, "LORD, it is nothing for You to help, whether with many or with those who have no power; help us, O LORD our God, for we rest on You, and in Your name we go against this multitude. O LORD, You are our God; do not let man prevail against You!"

2 CHRONICLES 14:11

Then Jehoshaphat stood in the assembly of Judah and Jerusalem, in the house of the LORD, before the new court, and said: "O LORD God of our fathers, are You not God in heaven, and do You not rule over all the kingdoms of the nations, and in Your hand is there not power and might, so that no one is able to withstand You? Are You not our God, who drove out the inhabitants of this land before Your people Israel, and gave it to the descendants of Abraham Your friend forever? And they dwell in it, and have built You a sanctuary in it for Your name, saying, 'If disaster comes upon us—sword, judgment, pestilence, or famine—we will stand before this temple and in Your presence (for Your name is in this temple), and cry out to You in our affliction, and You will hear and save.' And now, here are the people of Ammon, Moab, and Mount Seir—whom You would not let Israel invade when they came out of the land of Egypt, but they turned from them and did not destroy them—here they are, rewarding us by coming to throw us out of Your possession which You have given us to inherit. O our God, will You not judge them? For we have no power against this great multitude that is coming against us; nor do we know what to do, but our eyes are upon You."

2 CHRONICLES 20:5–12

When the righteous are in authority, the people
    rejoice;
But when a wicked man rules, the people groan.

PROVERBS 29:2

O Lord, though our iniquities testify
    against us,
Do it for Your name's sake;
For our backslidings are many,
We have sinned against You. . . .

We acknowledge, O Lord, our wickedness
And the iniquity of our fathers,
For we have sinned against You.

JEREMIAH 14:7, 20

We have sinned and committed iniquity, we have done wickedly and rebelled, even by departing from Your precepts and Your judgments. Neither have we heeded Your servants the prophets, who spoke in Your name to our kings and our princes, to our fathers and all the people of the land. O Lord, righteousness belongs to You, but to us shame of face, as it is this day—to the men of Judah, to the inhabitants of Jerusalem and all Israel, those near and those far off in all the countries to which You have driven them, because of the unfaithfulness which they have committed against You.

O Lord, to us belongs shame of face, to our kings, our princes, and our fathers, because we have sinned against You. To the Lord our God belong mercy and forgiveness, though we have rebelled against Him. We have not obeyed the voice of the LORD our God, to walk in His laws, which He set before us by His servants the prophets. Yes, all Israel has transgressed Your law, and has departed so as not to obey Your voice; therefore the curse and the oath written in the Law of Moses the servant of God have been poured out on us, because we have sinned against Him. And He has confirmed His words, which He spoke against us and against our judges who judged us, by bringing upon us a great disaster; for under the whole heaven such has never been done as what has been done to Jerusalem.

As it is written in the Law of Moses, all this disaster has come upon us; yet we have not made our prayer before the LORD our God, that we might turn from our iniquities and understand Your truth. Therefore the LORD has kept the disaster in mind, and brought it upon us; for the LORD our God is righteous in all the works which He does, though we have not obeyed His voice. And now, O Lord our God, who brought Your people out of the land of Egypt with a mighty hand, and made Yourself a name, as it is this day—we have sinned, we have done wickedly!

DANIEL 9:5–15

Brethren, my heart's desire and prayer to God for Israel is that they may be saved.

ROMANS 10:1

PRAYER FOR SPIRITUAL HEALING

When Elisha came into the house, there was the child, lying dead on his bed. He went in therefore, shut the door behind the two of them, and prayed to the Lord. And he went up and lay on the child, and put his mouth on his mouth, his eyes on his eyes, and his hands on his hands; and he stretched himself out on the child, and the flesh of the child became warm. He returned and walked back and forth in the house, and again went up and stretched himself out on him; then the child sneezed seven times, and the child opened his eyes. And he called Gehazi and said, "Call this Shunammite woman." So he called her. And when she came in to him, he said, "Pick up your son." So she went in, fell at his feet, and bowed to the ground; then she picked up her son and went out.

2 KINGS 4:32–37

"For there stood by me this night an angel of the God to whom I belong and whom I serve, saying, 'Do not be afraid, Paul; you must be brought before Caesar; and indeed God has granted you all those who sail with you.' Therefore take heart, men, for I believe God that it will be just as it was told me."

ACTS 27:23–25

Is anyone among you suffering? Let him pray. Is anyone cheerful? Let him sing psalms.

JAMES 5:13

> The Lord also will be a refuge for the
>   oppressed,
> A refuge in times of trouble.
> And those who know Your name will put their
>   trust in You;
> For You, Lord, have not forsaken those who
>   seek You.

PSALM 9:9–10

For I said in my haste,
"I am cut off from before Your eyes";
Nevertheless You heard the voice of my
supplications
When I cried out to You.

PSALM 31:22

In righteousness you shall be established;
You shall be far from oppression, for you shall
not fear;
And from terror, for it shall not come near you.

ISAIAH 54:14

For I know the thoughts that I think toward you, says the LORD, thoughts of peace and not of evil, to give you a future and a hope. Then you will call upon Me and go and pray to Me, and I will listen to you. And you will seek Me and find Me, when you search for Me with all your heart.

JEREMIAH 29:11–13

"Peace I leave with you, My peace I give to you; not as the world gives do I give to you. Let not your heart be troubled, neither let it be afraid."

JOHN 14:27

Grace to you and peace from God the Father and our Lord Jesus Christ, who gave Himself for our sins, that He might deliver us from this present evil age, according to the will of our God and Father.

GALATIANS 1:3–4

And be renewed in the spirit of your mind.

EPHESIANS 4:23

In my distress I called upon the LORD,
And cried out to my God;
He heard my voice from His temple,
And my cry entered His ears.

2 SAMUEL 22:7

He restores my soul;
He leads me in the paths of righteousness
For His name's sake.

Yea, though I walk through the valley of the
        shadow of death,
I will fear no evil;
For You are with me;
Your rod and Your staff, they comfort me.

PSALM 23:3–4

Then Jehoshaphat stood in the assembly of Judah and Jerusalem, in the house of the LORD, before the new court, and said: "O LORD God of our fathers, are You not God in heaven, and do You not rule over all the kingdoms of the nations, and in Your hand is there not power and might, so that no one is able to withstand You? Are You not our God, who drove out the inhabitants of this land before Your people Israel, and gave it to the descendants of Abraham Your friend forever? And they dwell in it, and have built You a sanctuary in it for Your name, saying, 'If disaster comes upon us—sword, judgment, pestilence, or famine—we will stand before this temple and in Your presence (for Your name is in this temple), and cry out to You in our affliction, and You will hear and save.' And now, here are the people of Ammon, Moab, and Mount Seir—whom You would not let Israel invade when they came out of the land of Egypt, but they turned from them and did not destroy them—here they are, rewarding us by coming to throw us out of Your possession which You have given us to inherit. O our God, will You not judge them? For we have no power against this great multitude that is coming

against us; nor do we know what to do, but our eyes
are upon You."

2 CHRONICLES 20:5–12

Therefore You delivered them into the hand of
      their enemies,
Who oppressed them;
And in the time of their trouble,
When they cried to You,
You heard from heaven;
And according to Your abundant mercies
You gave them deliverers who saved them
From the hand of their enemies.

But after they had rest,
They again did evil before You.
Therefore You left them in the hand of their
      enemies,
So that they had dominion over them;
Yet when they returned and cried out to You,
You heard from heaven;
And many times You delivered them according
      to Your mercies.

NEHEMIAH 9:27–28

Will God hear his cry
When trouble comes upon him?

JOB 27:9

Hear me when I call, O God of my
        righteousness!
You have relieved me in my distress;
Have mercy on me, and hear my prayer.

PSALM 4:1

In my distress I called upon the LORD,
And cried out to my God;
He heard my voice from His temple,
And my cry came before Him, even to His ears.

PSALM 18:6

My God, My God, why have You forsaken Me?
Why are You so far from helping Me,
And from the words of My groaning?

PSALM 22:1

They cried to You, and were delivered;
They trusted in You, and were not ashamed. . . .

For He has not despised nor abhorred the
      affliction of the afflicted;
Nor has He hidden His face from Him;
But when He cried to Him, He heard.

PSALM 22:5, 24

For this cause everyone who is godly shall pray
      to You
In a time when You may be found;
Surely in a flood of great waters
They shall not come near him.

PSALM 32:6

This poor man cried out, and the Lord
      heard him,
And saved him out of all his troubles.

PSALM 34:6

"Call upon Me in the day of trouble;
I will deliver you, and you shall glorify Me."

PSALM 50:15

Make haste, O God, to deliver me!
Make haste to help me, O Lord!

PSALM 70:1

You called in trouble, and I delivered you;
I answered you in the secret place of thunder;
I tested you at the waters of Meribah.

PSALM 81:7

Who knows the power of Your anger?
For as the fear of You, so is Your wrath.
So teach us to number our days,
That we may gain a heart of wisdom. . . .

And let the beauty of the LORD our God be
     upon us,
And establish the work of our hands for us;
Yes, establish the work of our hands.

PSALM 90:11–12, 17

He shall regard the prayer of the destitute,
And shall not despise their prayer.

PSALM 102:17

The LORD shall send the rod of Your strength
     out of Zion.
Rule in the midst of Your enemies!

PSALM 110:2

> "Many a time they have afflicted me from my
> youth;
> Yet they have not prevailed against me."

PSALM 129:2

And suddenly a great tempest arose on the sea, so that the boat was covered with the waves. But He was asleep. Then His disciples came to Him and awoke Him, saying, "Lord, save us! We are perishing!"

But He said to them, "Why are you fearful, O you of little faith?" Then He arose and rebuked the winds and the sea, and there was a great calm.

MATTHEW 8:24–26

Then Samson called to the LORD, saying, "O Lord GOD, remember me, I pray! Strengthen me, I pray, just this once, O God, that I may with one blow take vengeance on the Philistines for my two eyes!" And Samson took hold of the two middle pillars which supported the temple, and he braced himself against them, one on his right and the other on his left. Then Samson said, "Let me die with the Philistines!" And he pushed with all his might, and the temple fell on the lords and all the people who were in it. So the dead that he killed at his death were more than he had killed in his life.

And his brothers and all his father's household came down and took him, and brought him up and buried him between Zorah and Eshtaol in the tomb of his father Manoah. He had judged Israel twenty years.

JUDGES 16:28–31

Whenever I am afraid,
I will trust in You.
In God (I will praise His word),
In God I have put my trust;
I will not fear.
What can flesh do to me? . . .

In God I have put my trust;
I will not be afraid.
What can man do to me?

PSALM 56:3–4, 11

Do not be afraid of sudden terror,
Nor of trouble from the wicked when it comes;
For the LORD will be your confidence,
And will keep your foot from being caught.

PROVERBS 3:25–26

For God has not given us a spirit of fear, but of power and of love and of a sound mind.

2 TIMOTHY 1:7

There is no fear in love; but perfect love casts out fear, because fear involves torment. But he who fears has not been made perfect in love.

1 JOHN 4:18

You shall hide them in the secret place of Your
    presence
From the plots of man;
You shall keep them secretly in a pavilion
From the strife of tongues.

PSALM 31:20

He who dwells in the secret place of the Most
    High
Shall abide under the shadow of the Almighty.
I will say of the LORD, "He is my refuge and my
    fortress;
My God, in Him I will trust."

Surely He shall deliver you from the snare of the
    fowler

And from the perilous pestilence.
He shall cover you with His feathers,
And under His wings you shall take refuge;
His truth shall be your shield and buckler.
You shall not be afraid of the terror by night,
Nor of the arrow that flies by day,
Nor of the pestilence that walks in darkness,
Nor of the destruction that lays waste at
      noonday.

A thousand may fall at your side,
And ten thousand at your right hand;
But it shall not come near you.
Only with your eyes shall you look,
And see the reward of the wicked.

Because you have made the LORD, who is my
      refuge,
Even the Most High, your dwelling place,
No evil shall befall you,
Nor shall any plague come near your dwelling;
For He shall give His angels charge over you,
To keep you in all your ways.
In their hands they shall bear you up,
Lest you dash your foot against a stone.
You shall tread upon the lion and the cobra,

The young lion and the serpent you shall
    trample underfoot.

"Because he has set his love upon Me, therefore
    I will deliver him;
I will set him on high, because he has known
    My name.
He shall call upon Me, and I will answer him;
I will be with him in trouble;
I will deliver him and honor him.
With long life I will satisfy him,
And show him My salvation."

PSALM 91

You will keep him in perfect peace,
Whose mind is stayed on You,
Because he trusts in You.
Trust in the LORD forever,
For in YAH, the LORD, is everlasting strength.
For He brings down those who dwell on high,
The lofty city;
He lays it low,
He lays it low to the ground,
He brings it down to the dust.
The foot shall tread it down—

The feet of the poor
And the steps of the needy."

The way of the just is uprightness;
O Most Upright,
You weigh the path of the just.
Yes, in the way of Your judgments,
O Lord, we have waited for You;
The desire of our soul is for Your name
And for the remembrance of You.
With my soul I have desired You in the night,
Yes, by my spirit within me I will seek You
        early;
For when Your judgments are in the earth,
The inhabitants of the world will learn
        righteousness.

Let grace be shown to the wicked,
Yet he will not learn righteousness;
In the land of uprightness he will deal unjustly,
And will not behold the majesty of the Lord.
Lord, when Your hand is lifted up, they will
        not see.
But they will see and be ashamed
For their envy of people;
Yes, the fire of Your enemies shall devour them.

Lord, You will establish peace for us,
For You have also done all our works in us.
O Lord our God, masters besides You
Have had dominion over us;
But by You only we make mention of
      Your name.
They are dead, they will not live;
They are deceased, they will not rise.
Therefore You have punished and
      destroyed them,
And made all their memory to perish.
You have increased the nation, O Lord,
You have increased the nation;
You are glorified;
You have expanded all the borders of the land.

Lord, in trouble they have visited You,
They poured out a prayer when Your chastening
      was upon them.
As a woman with child
Is in pain and cries out in her pangs,
When she draws near the time of her delivery,
So have we been in Your sight, O Lord.
We have been with child, we have been in pain;
We have, as it were, brought forth wind;

We have not accomplished any deliverance in
      the earth,
Nor have the inhabitants of the world fallen.

Your dead shall live;
Together with my dead body they shall arise.
Awake and sing, you who dwell in dust;
For your dew is like the dew of herbs,
And the earth shall cast out the dead.

Come, my people, enter your chambers,
And shut your doors behind you;
Hide yourself, as it were, for a little moment,
Until the indignation is past.
For behold, the LORD comes out of His place
To punish the inhabitants of the earth for their
      iniquity;
The earth will also disclose her blood,
And will no more cover her slain.

ISAIAH 26:3–21

"No weapon formed against you shall prosper,
And every tongue which rises against you in
      judgment
You shall condemn.
This is the heritage of the servants of the LORD,

And their righteousness is from Me,"
Says the LORD.

ISAIAH 54:17

"Peace I leave with you, My peace I give to you; not as the world gives do I give to you. Let not your heart be troubled, neither let it be afraid."

JOHN 14:27

Now may the God of hope fill you with all joy and peace in believing, that you may abound in hope by the power of the Holy Spirit.

ROMANS 15:13

Finally, brethren, farewell. Become complete. Be of good comfort, be of one mind, live in peace; and the God of love and peace will be with you.

2 CORINTHIANS 13:11

Be anxious for nothing, but in everything by prayer and supplication, with thanksgiving, let your requests be made known to God; and the peace of God, which surpasses all understanding, will guard your hearts and minds through Christ Jesus.

PHILIPPIANS 4:6–7

Now may the Lord of peace Himself give you peace always in every way. The Lord be with you all.

2 THESSALONIANS 3:16

Now may the God of peace who brought up our Lord Jesus from the dead, that great Shepherd of the sheep, through the blood of the everlasting covenant, make you complete in every good work to do His will, working in you what is well pleasing in His sight, through Jesus Christ, to whom be glory forever and ever. Amen.

HEBREWS 13:20–21

Then we cried out to the LORD God of our fathers, and the LORD heard our voice and looked on our affliction and our labor and our oppression. So the LORD brought us out of Egypt with a mighty hand and with an outstretched arm, with great terror and with signs and wonders. He has brought us to this place and has given us this land, "a land flowing with milk and honey."

DEUTERONOMY 26:7–9

The LORD is my light and my salvation;
Whom shall I fear?

The Lord is the strength of my life;
Of whom shall I be afraid?
When the wicked came against me
To eat up my flesh,
My enemies and foes,
They stumbled and fell.
Though an army may encamp against me,
My heart shall not fear;
Though war may rise against me,
In this I will be confident.

PSALM 27:1–3

PRAYER FOR PHYSICAL HEALING

Then Jonah prayed to the Lord his God from the fish's belly. And he said:

"I cried out to the Lord because of my
    affliction,
And He answered me.

"Out of the belly of Sheol I cried,
And You heard my voice.
For You cast me into the deep,
Into the heart of the seas,
And the floods surrounded me;

All Your billows and Your waves passed
  over me.
Then I said, 'I have been cast out of Your sight;
Yet I will look again toward Your holy temple.'
The waters surrounded me, even to my soul;
The deep closed around me;
Weeds were wrapped around my head.
I went down to the moorings of the mountains;
The earth with its bars closed behind me
  forever;
Yet You have brought up my life from the pit,
O Lord, my God.

"When my soul fainted within me,
I remembered the Lord;
And my prayer went up to You,
Into Your holy temple.

"Those who regard worthless idols
Forsake their own Mercy.
But I will sacrifice to You
With the voice of thanksgiving;
I will pay what I have vowed.
Salvation is of the Lord."

JONAH 2:1–9

And Abraham said to God, "Oh, that Ishmael might live before You!"

Then God said: "No, Sarah your wife shall bear you a son, and you shall call his name Isaac; I will establish My covenant with him for an everlasting covenant, and with his descendants after him."

GENESIS 17:18–19

"Now therefore, stand and see this great thing which the LORD will do before your eyes."

1 SAMUEL 12:16

Then the king answered and said to the man of God, "Please entreat the favor of the LORD your God, and pray for me, that my hand may be restored to me."

So the man of God entreated the LORD, and the king's hand was restored to him, and became as before.

1 KINGS 13:6

Then he cried out to the LORD and said, "O LORD my God, have You also brought tragedy on the widow with whom I lodge, by killing her son?" And he stretched himself out on the child three times, and cried out to the LORD and said, "O LORD my God, I pray, let this child's soul come back to him." Then the LORD heard the voice of Elijah; and the soul of the child came back to him, and he revived.

And Elijah took the child and brought him down from the upper room into the house, and gave him to his mother. And Elijah said, "See, your son lives!"

Then the woman said to Elijah, "Now by this I know that you are a man of God, and that the word of the LORD in your mouth is the truth."

1 KINGS 17:20–24

In those days Hezekiah was sick and near death. And Isaiah the prophet, the son of Amoz, went to him and said to him, "Thus says the LORD: 'Set your house in order, for you shall die, and not live.' "

Then he turned his face toward the wall, and prayed to the LORD, saying, "Remember now, O LORD, I pray, how I have walked before You in truth and with a loyal heart, and have done what was good in Your sight." And Hezekiah wept bitterly.

2 KINGS 20:1–3

O LORD my God, I cried out to You,
And You healed me.

PSALM 30:2

He sent His word and healed them,
And delivered them from their destructions.

PSALM 107:20

Do not be wise in your own eyes;
Fear the LORD and depart from evil.
It will be health to your flesh,
And strength to your bones.

PROVERBS 3:7–8

Then as He entered a certain village, there met Him ten men who were lepers, who stood afar off. And they lifted up their voices and said, "Jesus, Master, have mercy on us!"

So when He saw them, He said to them, "Go, show yourselves to the priests." And so it was that as they went, they were cleansed.

LUKE 17:12–14

And when He had called His twelve disciples to Him, He gave them power over unclean spirits, to cast them out, and to heal all kinds of sickness and all kinds of disease.

MATTHEW 10:1

And to have power to heal sicknesses and to cast out demons.

MARK 3:15

Then they took away the stone from the place where the dead man was lying. And Jesus lifted up His eyes and said, "Father, I thank You that You have heard Me."

JOHN 11:41

And he took him by the right hand and lifted him up, and immediately his feet and ankle bones received strength.

ACTS 3:7

Also a multitude gathered from the surrounding cities to Jerusalem, bringing sick people and those who were tormented by unclean spirits, and they were all healed.

ACTS 5:16

And in Lystra a certain man without strength in his feet was sitting, a cripple from his mother's womb, who had never walked. This man heard Paul speaking. Paul, observing him intently and seeing that he had faith to be healed, said with a loud voice, "Stand up straight on your feet!" And he leaped and walked.

ACTS 14:8–10

But Peter put them all out, and knelt down and prayed. And turning to the body he said, "Tabitha, arise." And she opened her eyes, and when she saw Peter she sat up. Then he gave her his hand and lifted her up; and when he had called the saints and widows, he presented her alive. And it became known throughout all Joppa, and many believed on the Lord.

ACTS 9:40–42

Now it happened, as we went to prayer, that a certain slave girl possessed with a spirit of divination met us, who brought her masters much profit by fortune-telling. This girl followed Paul and us, and cried out, saying, "These men are the servants of the Most High God, who proclaim to us the way of salvation." And this she did for many days.

But Paul, greatly annoyed, turned and said to the spirit, "I command you in the name of Jesus Christ to come out of her." And he came out that very hour.

ACTS 16:16–18

Now God worked unusual miracles by the hands of Paul, so that even handkerchiefs or aprons were brought from his body to the sick, and the diseases left them and the evil spirits went out of them.

ACTS 19:11–12

And it happened that the father of Publius lay sick of a fever and dysentery. Paul went in to him and prayed, and he laid his hands on him and healed him.

ACTS 28:8

Is anyone among you sick? Let him call for the elders of the church, and let them pray over him, anointing him with oil in the name of the Lord.

JAMES 5:14

Also He said to me, "Prophesy to the breath, prophesy, son of man, and say to the breath, 'Thus says the LORD God: "Come from the four winds, O breath, and breathe on these slain, that they may live."'" So I prophesied as He commanded me, and breath came into them, and they lived, and stood upon their feet, an exceedingly great army.

EZEKIEL 37:9–10

GOD'S GIFT OF PROSPERITY

"May God Almighty bless you,
   And make you fruitful and multiply you,
   That you may be an assembly of peoples;
   And give you the blessing of Abraham,
   To you and your descendants with you,
   That you may inherit the land
   In which you are a stranger,
   Which God gave to Abraham."

So Isaac sent Jacob away, and he went to Padan Aram, to Laban the son of Bethuel the Syrian, the brother of Rebekah, the mother of Jacob and Esau.

Esau saw that Isaac had blessed Jacob and sent him away to Padan Aram to take himself a wife from there, and that as he blessed him he gave him a charge, saying, "You shall not take a wife from the daughters of Canaan," and that Jacob had obeyed his father and his mother and had gone to Padan Aram. Also Esau saw that the daughters of Canaan did not please his father Isaac. So Esau went to Ishmael and took Mahalath the daughter of Ishmael, Abraham's son, the sister of Nebajoth, to be his wife in addition to the wives he had.

Now Jacob went out from Beersheba and went toward Haran. So he came to a certain place and stayed there all night, because the sun had set. And he took one of the stones of that place and put it at his head, and he lay down in that place to sleep. Then he dreamed, and behold, a ladder was set up on the earth, and its top reached to heaven; and there the angels of God were ascending and descending on it.

And behold, the Lord stood above it and said: "I am the Lord God of Abraham your father and the God of Isaac; the land on which you lie I will give to you and your descendants."

GENESIS 28:3–13

Then Rachel and Leah answered and said to him, "Is there still any portion or inheritance for us in our father's house? Are we not considered strangers by him? For he has sold us, and also completely consumed our money. For all these riches which God has taken from our father are really ours and our children's; now then, whatever God has said to you, do it."

GENESIS 31:13–16

But the Lord was with Joseph and showed him mercy, and He gave him favor in the sight of the keeper of the prison. And the keeper of the prison committed to Joseph's hand all the prisoners who were in the prison; whatever they did there, it was his doing. The keeper of the prison did not look into anything that was under Joseph's authority, because the LORD was with him; and whatever he did, the LORD made it prosper.

GENESIS 39:21–23

Blessed shall be your basket and your kneading bowl.

Blessed shall you be when you come in, and blessed shall you be when you go out.

The LORD will cause your enemies who rise against you to be defeated before your face; they shall come out against you one way and flee before you seven ways.

The LORD will command the blessing on you in your storehouses and in all to which you set your hand, and He will bless you in the land which the Lord your God is giving you.

The LORD will establish you as a holy people to Himself, just as He has sworn to you, if you keep the commandments of the LORD your God and walk in His ways. Then all peoples of the earth shall see that you are called by the name of the LORD, and they shall be afraid of you. And the LORD will grant you plenty of goods, in the fruit of your body, in the increase of your livestock, and in the produce of your ground, in the land of which the LORD swore to your fathers to give you. The LORD will open to you His good treasure, the heavens, to give the rain to your land in its season, and to bless all the work of your hand. You shall lend to many nations, but you shall not borrow. And the Lord will make you the head and not the tail; you shall be above only, and not be beneath, if you heed the commandments of the LORD your God, which I command you today, and are careful to observe them. So you shall not turn aside from any of the words which I command you this day, to the right or the left, to go after other gods to serve them.

DEUTERONOMY 28:5–14

"Only be strong and very courageous, that you may observe to do according to all the law which Moses My servant commanded you; do not turn from it to the right hand or to the left, that you may prosper wherever you go. This Book of the Law shall not depart from your mouth, but you shall meditate in it day and night, that you may observe to do according to all that is written in it. For then you will make your way prosperous, and then you will have good success.

Have I not commanded you? Be strong and of good courage; do not be afraid, nor be dismayed, for the LORD your God is with you wherever you go."

JOSHUA 1:7–9

So Solomon answered all her questions; there was nothing so difficult for the king that he could not explain it to her. And when the queen of Sheba had seen all the wisdom of Solomon, the house that he had built, the food on his table, the seating of his servants, the service of his waiters and their apparel, his cupbearers, and his entryway by which he went up to the house of the LORD, there was no more spirit in her. Then she said to the king: "It was a true report which I heard in my own land about your words and your wisdom. However I did not believe the words until I came and saw with my own eyes; and indeed the half was not told me. Your wisdom and prosperity exceed the fame of which I heard."

1 KINGS 10:3–7

And when David had finished offering the burnt offerings and the peace offerings, he blessed the people in the name of the LORD.

1 CHRONICLES 16:2

And Hezekiah appointed the divisions of the priests and the Levites according to their divisions, each man according to his service, the priests and Levites for burnt offerings and peace offerings, to serve, to give thanks, and to praise in the gates of the camp of the Lord.

2 CHRONICLES 31:2

This same Hezekiah also stopped the water outlet of Upper Gihon, and brought the water by tunnel to the west side of the City of David. Hezekiah prospered in all his works.

2 CHRONICLES 32:30

And so it was, after the Lord had spoken these words to Job, that the Lord said to Eliphaz the Temanite, "My wrath is aroused against you and your two friends, for you have not spoken of Me what is right, as My servant Job has. Now therefore, take for yourselves seven bulls and seven rams, go to My servant Job, and offer up for yourselves a burnt offering; and My servant Job shall pray for you. For I will accept him, lest I deal with you according to your folly; because you have not spoken of Me what is right, as My servant Job has."

So Eliphaz the Temanite and Bildad the Shuhite and Zophar the Naamathite went and did as the LORD commanded them; for the LORD had accepted Job. And the LORD restored Job's losses when he prayed for his friends. Indeed the LORD gave Job twice as much as he had before.

JOB 42:7–10

He shall be like a tree
Planted by the rivers of water,
That brings forth its fruit in its season,
Whose leaf also shall not wither;
And whatever he does shall prosper.

PSALM 1:3

Now in my prosperity I said,
"I shall never be moved."
LORD, by Your favor You have made my
        mountain stand strong;
You hid Your face, and I was troubled.

I cried out to You, O LORD;
And to the LORD I made supplication.

PSALM 30:6–8

The LORD will give grace and glory;
No good thing will He withhold
From those who walk uprightly.

PSALM 84:11

He also brought them out with silver and gold,
And there was none feeble among His tribes.

PSALM 105:37

He raises the poor out of the dust,
And lifts the needy out of the ash heap,
That He may seat him with princes—
With the princes of His people.

PSALM 113:7–8

Do not be wise in your own eyes;
Fear the LORD and depart from evil.
It will be health to your flesh,
And strength to your bones.

Honor the LORD with your possessions,
And with the firstfruits of all your increase;
So your barns will be filled with plenty,
And your vats will overflow with new wine.

PROVERBS 3:7–10

He who gives to the poor will not lack,
But he who hides his eyes will have many curses.

PROVERBS 28:27

For what more has the wise man than the fool?
What does the poor man have,
Who knows how to walk before the living?

ECCLESIASTES 6:8

Cast your bread upon the waters,
For you will find it after many days.

ECCLESIASTES 11:1

"I will give you the treasures of darkness
And hidden riches of secret places,
That you may know that I, the LORD,
Who call you by your name,
Am the God of Israel."

ISAIAH 45:3

"Then you shall delight yourself in the LORD;
And I will cause you to ride on the high hills of
the earth,

And feed you with the heritage of Jacob your
    father.
The mouth of the Lord has spoken."

ISAIAH 58:14

"But I will gather the remnant of My flock out of all countries where I have driven them, and bring them back to their folds; and they shall be fruitful and increase. I will set up shepherds over them who will feed them; and they shall fear no more, nor be dismayed, nor shall they be lacking," says the Lord.

"Behold, the days are coming," says the Lord,
"That I will raise to David a Branch of
    righteousness;
A King shall reign and prosper,
And execute judgment and righteousness in the
    earth.
In His days Judah will be saved,
And Israel will dwell safely;
Now this is His name by which He will be called:

THE LORD OUR RIGHTEOUSNESS.

"Therefore, behold, the days are coming," says the Lord, "that they shall no longer say, 'As the Lord lives who brought up the children of Israel from the land of Egypt,' but, 'As the Lord lives who brought up and led the descendants of the house of Israel from the north country and from all the countries where I had driven them.' And they shall dwell in their own land."

JEREMIAH 23:3-8

So this Daniel prospered in the reign of Darius and in the reign of Cyrus the Persian.

DANIEL 6:28

So Jesus answered and said, "Assuredly, I say to you, there is no one who has left house or brothers or sisters or father or mother or wife or children or lands, for My sake and the gospel's, who shall not receive a hundredfold now in this time—houses and brothers and sisters and mothers and children and lands, with persecutions—and in the age to come, eternal life. But many who are first will be last, and the last first."

MARK 10:29-31

"But seek first the kingdom of God and His righteousness, and all these things shall be added to you."

MATTHEW 6:33

For you know the grace of our Lord Jesus Christ, that though He was rich, yet for your sakes He became poor, that you through His poverty might become rich.

2 CORINTHIANS 8:9

And my God shall supply all your need according to His riches in glory by Christ Jesus.

PHILIPPIANS 4:19

Then He took the five loaves and the two fish, and looking up to heaven, He blessed and broke them, and gave them to the disciples to set before the multitude.

LUKE 9:16

And Jesus took the loaves, and when He had given thanks He distributed them to the disciples, and the disciples to those sitting down; and likewise of the fish, as much as they wanted.

JOHN 6:11

Command those who are rich in this present age not to be haughty, nor to trust in uncertain riches but in the living God, who gives us richly all things to enjoy.

1 TIMOTHY 6:17

Beloved, I pray that you may prosper in all things and be in health, just as your soul prospers.

3 JOHN 1:2

> Ask the LORD for rain
> In the time of the latter rain.
> The LORD will make flashing clouds;
> He will give them showers of rain,
> Grass in the field for everyone.

ZECHARIAH 10:1

Then Elijah said to Ahab, "Go up, eat and drink; for there is the sound of abundance of rain." So Ahab went up to eat and drink. And Elijah went up to the top of Carmel; then he bowed down on the ground, and put his face between his knees, and said to his servant, "Go up now, look toward the sea."

So he went up and looked, and said, "There is nothing." And seven times he said, "Go again."

Then it came to pass the seventh time, that he said, "There is a cloud, as small as a man's hand, rising out of the sea!" So he said, "Go up, say to Ahab, 'Prepare your chariot, and go down before the rain stops you.'"

Now it happened in the meantime that the sky

became black with clouds and wind, and there was a heavy rain. So Ahab rode away and went to Jezreel. Then the hand of the LORD came upon Elijah; and he girded up his loins and ran ahead of Ahab to the entrance of Jezreel.

1 KINGS 18:41–46

"Then I will give you rain in its season, the land shall yield its produce, and the trees of the field shall yield their fruit.

Your threshing shall last till the time of vintage, and the vintage shall last till the time of sowing;

you shall eat your bread to the full, and dwell in your land safely."

LEVITICUS 26:4–5

PROMISE OF REVIVAL

But when He saw the multitudes, He was moved with compassion for them, because they were weary and scattered, like sheep having no shepherd. Then He said to His disciples, "The harvest truly is plentiful, but the laborers are few. Therefore pray the Lord of the harvest to send out laborers into His harvest."

MATTHEW 9:36–38

And many of the Samaritans of that city believed in Him because of the word of the woman who testified, "He told me all that I ever did." So when the Samaritans had come to Him, they urged Him to stay with them; and He stayed there two days. And many more believed because of His own word.

Then they said to the woman, "Now we believe, not because of what you said, for we ourselves have heard Him and we know that this is indeed the Christ, the Savior of the world."

JOHN 4:35–42

Restore to me the joy of Your salvation,
And uphold me by Your generous Spirit.
Then I will teach transgressors Your ways,
And sinners shall be converted to You.

PSALM 51:12–13

That Your people may rejoice in You?

PSALM 85:6

It is time for You to act, O LORD,
For they have regarded Your law as void.

PSALM 119:126

"Call to Me, and I will answer you, and show you great and mighty things, which you do not know."

JEREMIAH 33:3

"When I shut up heaven and there is no rain, or command the locusts to devour the land, or send pestilence among My people, if My people who are called by My name will humble themselves, and pray and seek My face, and turn from their wicked ways, then I will hear from heaven, and will forgive their sin and heal their land."

2 CHRONICLES 7:13–14

Be glad then, you children of Zion,
And rejoice in the LORD your God;
For He has given you the former rain faithfully,
And He will cause the rain to come down
       for you—
The former rain,
And the latter rain in the first month.
The threshing floors shall be full of wheat,
And the vats shall overflow with new wine
       and oil.

"So I will restore to you the years that the
        swarming locust has eaten,
The crawling locust,
The consuming locust,
And the chewing locust,
My great army which I sent among you.
You shall eat in plenty and be satisfied,
And praise the name of the LORD your God,
Who has dealt wondrously with you;
And My people shall never be put to shame.
Then you shall know that I am in the midst of
        Israel:
I am the LORD your God
And there is no other.
My people shall never be put to shame.

"And it shall come to pass afterward
That I will pour out My Spirit on all flesh;
Your sons and your daughters shall prophesy,
Your old men shall dream dreams,
Your young men shall see visions.
And also on My menservants and on My
        maidservants
I will pour out My Spirit in those days."

JOEL 2:23–29

"The Spirit of the Lord God is upon Me,
Because the LORD has anointed Me
To preach good tidings to the poor;
He has sent Me to heal the brokenhearted,
To proclaim liberty to the captives,
And the opening of the prison to those who are
    bound; . . .

But you shall be named the priests of the LORD,
They shall call you the servants of our God.
You shall eat the riches of the Gentiles,
And in their glory you shall boast."

ISAIAH 61:1, 6

A prayer of Habakkuk the prophet, on Shigionoth.

O LORD, I have heard Your speech and was
    afraid;
O LORD, revive Your work in the midst of the
    years!
In the midst of the years make it known;
In wrath remember mercy.

God came from Teman,
The Holy One from Mount Paran. *Selah*

His glory covered the heavens,

And the earth was full of His praise.

HABAKKUK 3:1–3

And He Himself is the propitiation for our sins, and not for ours only but also for the whole world.

1 JOHN 2:2

PRAYER FOR GUIDANCE

"Call upon Me in the day of trouble;
I will deliver you, and you shall glorify Me."

PSALM 50:15

When I cry out to You,
Then my enemies will turn back;
This I know, because God is for me.

PSALM 56:9

Trust in Him at all times, you people;
Pour out your heart before Him;
God is a refuge for us.

PSALM 62:8

Lead me, O LORD, in Your righteousness
because of my enemies;

Make Your way straight before my face.

PSALM 5:8

He makes me to lie down in green pastures;
He leads me beside the still waters.

PSALM 23:2

Lead me in Your truth and teach me,
For You are the God of my salvation;
On You I wait all the day. . . .

The humble He guides in justice,
And the humble He teaches His way.

PSALM 25:5, 9

Teach me Your way, O Lord,
And lead me in a smooth path, because of my
     enemies.

PSALM 27:11

For this is God,
Our God forever and ever;
He will be our guide
Even to death.

PSALM 48:14

Therefore David inquired of the LORD, saying, "Shall I go and attack these Philistines?"

And the LORD said to David, "Go and attack the Philistines, and save Keilah." . . .

Then David said, "O LORD God of Israel, Your servant has certainly heard that Saul seeks to come to Keilah to destroy the city for my sake. Will the men of Keilah deliver me into his hand? Will Saul come down, as Your servant has heard? O LORD God of Israel, I pray, tell Your servant."

And the LORD said, "He will come down."

Then David said, "Will the men of Keilah deliver me and my men into the hand of Saul?"

And the LORD said, "They will deliver you."

And David stayed in strongholds in the wilderness, and remained in the mountains in the Wilderness of Ziph. Saul sought him every day, but God did not deliver him into his hand.

1 SAMUEL 23:2, 10−12, 14

"Then you shall call, and the LORD will answer;
You shall cry, and He will say, 'Here I am.'

"If you take away the yoke from your midst,

The pointing of the finger, and speaking
    wickedness,
If you extend your soul to the hungry
And satisfy the afflicted soul,
Then your light shall dawn in the darkness,
And your darkness shall be as the noonday.
The LORD will guide you continually,
And satisfy your soul in drought,
And strengthen your bones;
You shall be like a watered garden,
And like a spring of water, whose waters do
    not fail."

ISAIAH 58:9–11

When they heard the king, they departed; and behold, the star which they had seen in the East went before them, till it came and stood over where the young Child was.

MATTHEW 2:9

You will guide me with Your counsel,
And afterward receive me to glory.

PSALM 73:24

In the daytime also He led them with the cloud,
And all the night with a light of fire.

PSALM 78:14

Teach me, O LORD, the way of Your statutes,
And I shall keep it to the end.

PSALM 119:33

Teach me to do Your will,
For You are my God;
Your Spirit is good.
Lead me in the land of uprightness.

PSALM 143:10

"I will bring the blind by a way they did
        not know;
I will lead them in paths they have not known.
I will make darkness light before them,
And crooked places straight.
These things I will do for them,
And not forsake them."

ISAIAH 42:16

"Be strong and of good courage, do not fear nor be afraid of them; for the LORD your God, He is the One who goes with you. He will not leave you nor forsake you."

DEUTERONOMY 31:6

Then the children of Israel went up and wept before the LORD until evening, and asked counsel of the LORD, saying, "Shall I again draw near for battle against the children of my brother Benjamin?"

And the LORD said, "Go up against him."

So the children of Israel approached the children of Benjamin on the second day. And Benjamin went out against them from Gibeah on the second day, and cut down to the ground eighteen thousand more of the children of Israel; all these drew the sword.

Then all the children of Israel, that is, all the people, went up and came to the house of God and wept. They sat there before the LORD and fasted that day until evening; and they offered burnt offerings and peace offerings before the LORD. So the children of Israel inquired of the LORD (the ark of the covenant of God was there in those days, and Phinehas the son of Eleazar, the son of Aaron, stood before it in those days), saying, "Shall I yet again go out to battle against the children of my brother Benjamin, or shall I cease?"

And the Lord said, "Go up, for tomorrow I will deliver them into your hand."

JUDGES 20:23–28

And the Lord called Samuel again the third time. So he arose and went to Eli, and said, "Here I am, for you did call me."

Then Eli perceived that the Lord had called the boy. Therefore Eli said to Samuel, "Go, lie down; and it shall be, if He calls you, that you must say, 'Speak, Lord, for Your servant hears.'" So Samuel went and lay down in his place.

Now the Lord came and stood and called as at other times, "Samuel! Samuel!"

And Samuel answered, "Speak, for Your servant hears."

1 SAMUEL 3:8–10

PREPARATION FOR PRAYER

May I suggest as you prepare yourself to come before the Father in prayer, that you meditate on God's Word and select scriptures that will prepare you mind and heart to communicate with the Lord. I have chosen Psalm 19:14 as my favorite verse to prepare my heart for prayer. It states, "Let the words of my mouth and the meditation of my heart be acceptable in Your sight, O LORD, my strength and my Redeemer." This verse prepares my heart and mind to come to the Father in a humble, repentant way. Why don't you select a scripture that will help you prepare for prayer?

MEDITATION IN GOD'S WORD

"This Book of the Law shall not depart from your mouth, but you shall meditate in it day and night, that you may observe to do according to all that is written in it. For then you will make your way prosperous, and then you will have good success."

JOSHUA 1:8

Blessed is the man
Who walks not in the counsel of the ungodly,
Nor stands in the path of sinners,
Nor sits in the seat of the scornful;
But his delight is in the law of the LORD,
And in His law he meditates day and night.
He shall be like a tree
Planted by the rivers of water,
That brings forth its fruit in its season,
Whose leaf also shall not wither;
And whatever he does shall prosper.

PSALM 1:1–3

Give ear to my words, O LORD,
Consider my meditation.
Give heed to the voice of my cry,
My King and my God,
For to You I will pray.
My voice You shall hear in the morning,
    O LORD;
In the morning I will direct it to You,

And I will look up.

PSALM 5:1–3

Let the words of my mouth and the meditation
    of my heart
Be acceptable in Your sight,
O Lord, my strength and my Redeemer.

PSALM 19:14

My mouth shall speak wisdom,
And the meditation of my heart shall give
    understanding.

PSALM 49:3

When I remember You on my bed,
I meditate on You in the night watches.
Because You have been my help,
Therefore in the shadow of Your wings I will
    rejoice.
My soul follows close behind You;
Your right hand upholds me.

PSALM 63:6–8

I will also meditate on all Your work,
And talk of Your deeds.

Your way, O God, is in the sanctuary;
Who is so great a God as our God?
You are the God who does wonders;
You have declared Your strength among the
       peoples.
You have with Your arm redeemed Your people,
The sons of Jacob and Joseph.

PSALM 77:12–15

I will sing to the LORD as long as I live;
I will sing praise to my God while I have my
       being.
May my meditation be sweet to Him;
I will be glad in the LORD.

PSALM 104:33–34

I will meditate on Your precepts,
And contemplate Your ways.
I will delight myself in Your statutes;
I will not forget Your word. . . .

Princes also sit and speak against me,
But Your servant meditates on Your statutes.
Your testimonies also are my delight
And my counselors.

My soul clings to the dust;
Revive me according to Your word.

PSALM 119:15–16, 23–25

My hands also I will lift up to Your
      commandments,
Which I love,
And I will meditate on Your statutes. . . .

Let Your tender mercies come to me, that I
      may live;
For Your law is my delight.
Let the proud be ashamed,
For they treated me wrongfully with falsehood;
But I will meditate on Your precepts.

PSALM 119:48, 77–78

Oh, how I love Your law!
It is my meditation all the day.
You, through Your commandments, make me
      wiser than my enemies;
For they are ever with me.
I have more understanding than all my
      teachers,

For Your testimonies are my meditation.

PSALM 119:97–99

I cry out with my whole heart;
Hear me, O Lord!
I will keep Your statutes.
I cry out to You;
Save me, and I will keep Your testimonies.
I rise before the dawning of the morning,
And cry for help;
I hope in Your word.
My eyes are awake through the night watches,
That I may meditate on Your word.
Hear my voice according to Your
lovingkindness;
O Lord, revive me according to Your justice.

PSALM 119:145–149

I remember the days of old;
I meditate on all Your works;
I muse on the work of Your hands.

PSALM 143:5

Finally, brethren, whatever things are true, whatever
things are noble, whatever things are just, whatever

things are pure, whatever things are lovely, whatever things are of good report, if there is any virtue and if there is anything praiseworthy—meditate on these things. The things which you learned and received and heard and saw in me, these do, and the God of peace will be with you.

PHILIPPIANS 4:8–9

Till I come, give attention to reading, to exhortation, to doctrine. Do not neglect the gift that is in you, which was given to you by prophecy with the laying on of the hands of the eldership. Meditate on these things; give yourself entirely to them, that your progress may be evident to all. Take heed to yourself and to the doctrine. Continue in them, for in doing this you will save both yourself and those who hear you.

1 TIMOTHY 4:13–16

MINISTERING TO GOD

But Samuel ministered before the LORD, even as a child, wearing a linen ephod.

1 SAMUEL 2:18

Now the boy Samuel ministered to the LORD before

Eli. And the word of the LORD was rare in those days; there was no widespread revelation.

1 SAMUEL 3:1

They were ministering with music before the dwelling place of the tabernacle of meeting, until Solomon had built the house of the LORD in Jerusalem, and they served in their office according to their order.

1 CHRONICLES 6:32

"Because they ministered to them before their idols and caused the house of Israel to fall into iniquity, therefore I have raised My hand in an oath against them," says the Lord GOD, "that they shall bear their iniquity. And they shall not come near Me to minister to Me as priest, nor come near any of My holy things, nor into the Most Holy Place; but they shall bear their shame and their abominations which they have committed. Nevertheless I will make them keep charge of the temple, for all its work, and for all that has to be done in it.

"But the priests, the Levites, the sons of Zadok, who kept charge of My sanctuary when the children of Israel went astray from Me, they shall come near Me to minister to Me; and they shall stand before Me to offer to Me the fat and the blood," says the Lord God. "They shall enter My sanctuary, and they shall come near My table to minister to Me, and they shall keep My charge."

EZEKIEL 44:12–16

"And the King will answer and say to them, 'Assuredly, I say to you, inasmuch as you did it to one of the least of these My brethren, you did it to Me.'"

MATTHEW 25:40

As they ministered to the Lord and fasted, the Holy Spirit said, "Now separate to Me Barnabas and Saul for the work to which I have called them."

ACTS 13:2

For God is not unjust to forget your work and labor of love which you have shown toward His name, in that you have ministered to the saints, and do minister.

HEBREWS 6:10

FASTING

Then I proclaimed a fast there at the river of Ahava, that we might humble ourselves before our God, to seek from Him the right way for us and our little ones and all our possessions. For I was ashamed to request of the king an escort of soldiers and horsemen to help us against the enemy on the road, because we had spoken to the king, saying, "The hand of our God is upon all those for good who seek Him, but His power and His wrath are against all those who forsake Him." So we fasted and entreated our God for this, and He answered our prayer.

EZRA 8:21–23

Then Ezra rose up from before the house of God, and went into the chamber of Jehohanan the son of Eliashib; and when he came there, he ate no bread and drank no water, for he mourned because of the guilt of those from the captivity.

EZRA 10:6

So it was, when I heard these words, that I sat down and wept, and mourned for many days; I was fasting and praying before the God of heaven.

NEHEMIAH 1:4

Go, gather all the Jews who are present in Shushan,
and fast for me; neither eat nor drink for three days,
night or day. My maids and I will fast likewise. And
so I will go to the king, which is against the law; and
if I perish, I perish!

ESTHER 4:16

Man is also chastened with pain on his bed,
And with strong pain in many of his bones,
So that his life abhors bread,
And his soul succulent food.

JOB 33:19–20

When I wept and chastened my soul with
fasting,
That became my reproach.

PSALM 69:10

My heart is stricken and withered like grass,
So that I forget to eat my bread.

PSALM 102:4

"Is this not the fast that I have chosen:
To loose the bonds of wickedness,

To undo the heavy burdens,
To let the oppressed go free,
And that you break every yoke?"

ISAIAH 58:6

Then I set my face toward the LORD GOD to make request by prayer and supplications, with fasting, sackcloth, and ashes. . . .

Now while I was speaking, praying, and confessing my sin and the sin of my people Israel, and presenting my supplication before the LORD my God for the holy mountain of my God, yes, while I was speaking in prayer, the man Gabriel, whom I had seen in the vision at the beginning, being caused to fly swiftly, reached me about the time of the evening offering. And he informed me, and talked with me, and said, "O Daniel, I have now come forth to give you skill to understand. At the beginning of your supplications the command went out, and I have come to tell you, for you are greatly beloved; therefore consider the matter, and understand the vision."

DANIEL 9:3, 20–23

Blow the trumpet in Zion,
Consecrate a fast,

Call a sacred assembly.

JOEL 2:15

So the people of Nineveh believed God, proclaimed a fast, and put on sackcloth, from the greatest to the least of them. . . .

Then God saw their works, that they turned from their evil way; and God relented from the disaster that He had said He would bring upon them, and He did not do it.

JONAH 3:5, 10

And when He had fasted forty days and forty nights, afterward He was hungry.

MATTHEW 4:2

"Moreover, when you fast, do not be like the hypocrites, with a sad countenance. For they disfigure their faces that they may appear to men to be fasting. Assuredly, I say to you, they have their reward."

MATTHEW 6:16

And Jesus said to them, "Can the friends of the bridegroom mourn as long as the bridegroom is with them?

But the days will come when the bridegroom will be taken away from them, and then they will fast."

MATTHEW 9:15

Then, having fasted and prayed, and laid hands on them, they sent them away.

ACTS 13:3

So when they had appointed elders in every church, and prayed with fasting, they commended them to the Lord in whom they had believed.

ACTS 14:23

Do not deprive one another except with consent for a time, that you may give yourselves to fasting and prayer; and come together again so that Satan does not tempt you because of your lack of self-control.

1 CORINTHIANS 7:5

In weariness and toil, in sleeplessness often, in hunger and thirst, in fastings often, in cold and nakedness— besides the other things, what comes upon me daily: my deep concern for all the churches.

2 CORINTHIANS 11:27–28

So he was there with the LORD forty days and forty nights; he neither ate bread nor drank water. And He wrote on the tablets the words of the covenant, the Ten Commandments.

EXODUS 34:28

When I went up into the mountain to receive the tablets of stone, the tablets of the covenant which the LORD made with you, then I stayed on the mountain forty days and forty nights. I neither ate bread nor drank water.

DEUTERONOMY 9:9

David therefore pleaded with God for the child, and David fasted and went in and lay all night on the ground. So the elders of his house arose and went to him, to raise him up from the ground. But he would not, nor did he eat food with them.

2 SAMUEL 12:16–17

PRAISE

Indeed it came to pass, when the trumpeters and singers were as one, to make one sound to be heard in praising and thanking the LORD, and when they lifted up their voice with the trumpets and cymbals and instruments of music, and praised the LORD, saying:

"For He is good,
For His mercy endures forever,"
that the house, the house of the LORD, was filled with a cloud, so that the priests could not continue ministering because of the cloud; for the glory of the LORD filled the house of God.

2 CHRONICLES 5:13–14

But let all those rejoice who put their trust
in You;
Let them ever shout for joy, because You
defend them;
Let those also who love Your name
Be joyful in You.

PSALM 5:11

I will praise You, O LORD, with my whole heart;
I will tell of all Your marvelous works.
I will be glad and rejoice in You;
I will sing praise to Your name, O Most High.

PSALM 9:1–2

I will sing to the LORD,
Because He has dealt bountifully with me.

PSALM 13:6

I will call upon the LORD, who is worthy to be
    praised;
So shall I be saved from my enemies.

PSALM 18:3

Therefore I will give thanks to You, O LORD,
    among the Gentiles,
And sing praises to Your name.

PSALM 18:49

But You are holy,
Enthroned in the praises of Israel.

PSALM 22:3

I will declare Your name to My brethren;
In the midst of the assembly I will praise You.

PSALM 22:22

Give unto the LORD the glory due to His name;
Worship the LORD in the beauty of holiness.

PSALM 29:2

Be glad in the LORD and rejoice, you righteous;
And shout for joy, all you upright in heart!

PSALM 32:11

Rejoice in the LORD, O you righteous!
For praise from the upright is beautiful.

PSALM 33:1

I will bless the LORD at all times;
His praise shall continually be in my mouth.

PSALM 34:1

I will give You thanks in the great assembly;
I will praise You among many people.

PSALM 35:18

Let them shout for joy and be glad,
Who favor my righteous cause;
And let them say continually,
"Let the LORD be magnified,
Who has pleasure in the prosperity of His
    servant."

PSALM 35:27

And my tongue shall speak of Your
     righteousness
And of Your praise all the day long.

PSALM 35:28

He has put a new song in my mouth—
Praise to our God;
Many will see it and fear,
And will trust in the LORD.

PSALM 40:3

Why are you cast down, O my soul?
And why are you disquieted within me?
Hope in God;
For I shall yet praise Him,
The help of my countenance and my God.

PSALM 42:11

In God we boast all day long,
And praise Your name forever.

PSALM 44:8

Oh, clap your hands, all you peoples!
Shout to God with the voice of triumph!

PSALM 47:1

Sing praises to God, sing praises!
Sing praises to our King, sing praises!

PSALM 47:6

Great is the LORD, and greatly to be praised
In the city of our God,
In His holy mountain.

PSALM 48:1

"Whoever offers praise glorifies Me;
And to him who orders his conduct aright
I will show the salvation of God."

PSALM 50:23

I will praise You forever,
Because You have done it;
And in the presence of Your saints
I will wait on Your name, for it is good.

PSALM 52:9

I will freely sacrifice to You;
I will praise Your name, O LORD, for it is good.

PSALM 54:6

In God (I will praise His word),
In God I have put my trust;
I will not fear.
What can flesh do to me?

PSALM 56:4

In God (I will praise His word),
In the Lord (I will praise His word).

PSALM 56:10

Vows made to You are binding upon me, O God;
I will render praises to You.

PSALM 56:12

My heart is steadfast, O God, my heart is steadfast;
I will sing and give praise.

PSALM 57:7

I will praise You, O Lord, among the peoples;
I will sing to You among the nations.

PSALM 57:9

Because Your lovingkindness is better than life,
My lips shall praise You.

PSALM 63:3

Thus I will bless You while I live;
I will lift up my hands in Your name.

PSALM 63:4

Sing out the honor of His name;
Make His praise glorious.

PSALM 66:2

Oh, bless our God, you peoples!
And make the voice of His praise to be heard.

PSALM 66:8

Let the peoples praise You, O God;
Let all the peoples praise You.

PSALM 67:3

Blessed be the Lord,
Who daily loads us with benefits,
The God of our salvation!

PSALM 68:19

I will praise the name of God with a song,
And will magnify Him with thanksgiving.

PSALM 69:30

Let my mouth be filled with Your praise
And with Your glory all the day.

PSALM 71:8

But I will hope continually,
And will praise You yet more and more.

PSALM 71:14

Oh, do not let the oppressed return ashamed!
Let the poor and needy praise Your name.

PSALM 74:21

So we, Your people and sheep of Your pasture,
Will give You thanks forever;
We will show forth Your praise to all
        generations.

PSALM 79:13

Who can utter the mighty acts of the LORD?
Who can declare all His praise?

PSALM 106:2

Then they believed His words;
They sang His praise.

PSALM 106:12

Oh, that men would give thanks to the LORD for
    His goodness,
And for His wonderful works to the children
    of men!

PSALM 107:8

From the rising of the sun to its going down
The LORD's name is to be praised.

PSALM 113:3

My lips shall utter praise,
For You teach me Your statutes.

PSALM 119:171

Lift up your hands in the sanctuary,
And bless the LORD.

PSALM 134:2

I will praise You with my whole heart;
Before the gods I will sing praises to You.

PSALM 138:1

I will extol You, my God, O King;
And I will bless Your name forever and ever.
Every day I will bless You,

And I will praise Your name forever and ever.
Great is the LORD, and greatly to be praised;
And His greatness is unsearchable.

PSALM 145:1–3

My mouth shall speak the praise of the LORD,
And all flesh shall bless His holy name
Forever and ever.

PSALM 145:21

Praise the LORD!
For it is good to sing praises to our God;
For it is pleasant, and praise is beautiful.

PSALM 147:1

Sing to the LORD with thanksgiving;
Sing praises on the harp to our God.

PSALM 147:7

Praise the LORD!

Sing to the LORD a new song,
And His praise in the assembly of saints.

PSALM 149:1

Praise the Lord!

Praise God in His sanctuary;
Praise Him in His mighty firmament!

Praise Him for His mighty acts;
Praise Him according to His excellent
greatness!

PSALM 150:1–2

Let everything that has breath praise the Lord.
Praise the Lord!

PSALM 150:6

O Lord, You are my God.
I will exalt You,
I will praise Your name,
For You have done wonderful things;
Your counsels of old are faithfulness and truth.

ISAIAH 25:1

And one of them, when he saw that he was healed,
returned, and with a loud voice glorified God, and fell
down on his face at His feet, giving Him thanks. And
he was a Samaritan.

LUKE 17:15–16

And immediately he received his sight, and followed Him, glorifying God. And all the people, when they saw it, gave praise to God.

LUKE 18:43

Then, as He was now drawing near the descent of the Mount of Olives, the whole multitude of the disciples began to rejoice and praise God with a loud voice for all the mighty works they had seen, saying:

> "'Blessed is the King who comes in the name of
> the LORD!'
> Peace in heaven and glory in the highest!"

LUKE 19:37–38

And they worshiped Him, and returned to Jerusalem with great joy, and were continually in the temple praising and blessing God.

LUKE 24:52–53

So continuing daily with one accord in the temple, and breaking bread from house to house, they ate their food with gladness and simplicity of heart, praising God and having favor with all the people.

And the Lord added to the church daily those who were being saved.

ACTS 2:46–47

So he, leaping up, stood and walked and entered the temple with them—walking, leaping, and praising God.

ACTS 3:8

But at midnight Paul and Silas were praying and singing hymns to God, and the prisoners were listening to them.

ACTS 16:25

But you are a chosen generation, a royal priesthood, a holy nation, His own special people, that you may proclaim the praises of Him who called you out of darkness into His marvelous light.

1 PETER 2:9

Then a voice came from the throne, saying, "Praise our God, all you His servants and those who fear Him, both small and great!"

REVELATION 19:5

O Lord, open my lips,
And my mouth shall show forth Your praise.

PSALM 51:15

THANKSGIVING

Oh, give thanks to the LORD!
Call upon His name;
Make known His deeds among the peoples!

1 CHRONICLES 16:8

So I brought the leaders of Judah up on the wall, and appointed two large thanksgiving choirs. One went to the right hand on the wall toward the Refuse Gate.

NEHEMIAH 12:31

Offer to God thanksgiving,
And pay your vows to the Most High.

PSALM 50:14

Make a joyful shout to the LORD, all you lands!
Serve the LORD with gladness;
Come before His presence with singing.
Know that the LORD, He is God;

It is He who has made us, and not we ourselves;
We are His people and the sheep of His pasture.

Enter into His gates with thanksgiving,
And into His courts with praise.
Be thankful to Him, and bless His name.

PSALM 100:1–4

I will offer to You the sacrifice of thanksgiving,
And will call upon the name of the LORD.

PSALM 116:17

Oh, give thanks to the God of heaven!
For His mercy endures forever.

PSALM 136:26

In everything give thanks; for this is the will of God
in Christ Jesus for you.

1 THESSALONIANS 5:18

For every creature of God is good, and nothing is to
be refused if it is received with thanksgiving.

1 TIMOTHY 4:4

Therefore by Him let us continually offer the sacrifice of praise to God, that is, the fruit of our lips, giving thanks to His name.

HEBREWS 13:15

And were continually in the temple praising and blessing God. Amen.

LUKE 24:53

Speaking to one another in psalms and hymns and spiritual songs, singing and making melody in your heart to the Lord, giving thanks always for all things to God the Father in the name of our Lord Jesus Christ.

EPHESIANS 5:19–20

Continue earnestly in prayer, being vigilant in it with thanksgiving.

COLOSSIANS 4:2

ATTITUDES FOR PRAYER

When we come to the Lord in prayer our attitude is very important. We are to confess our sins and have a repentant heart. We are entering God's presence and should do so with humility, adoration, and praise if we want Him to hear our prayers. The Lord is waiting for us to come to Him. When we come to Him, our attitude should be one of humility and sincere obedience to His Word.

FORGIVENESS

You have also given me the necks of my enemies,
So that I destroyed those who hated me.
They looked, but there was none to save;
Even to the LORD, but He did not answer
them. . . .

It is God who avenges me,
And subdues the peoples under me.

2 SAMUEL 22:41–42, 48

"For if you forgive men their trespasses, your heavenly Father will also forgive you."

MATTHEW 6:14

"And whenever you stand praying, if you have anything against anyone, forgive him, that your Father in heaven may also forgive you your trespasses. But if you do not forgive, neither will your Father in heaven forgive your trespasses."

MARK 11:25–26

Then Jesus said, "Father, forgive them, for they do not know what they do."

And they divided His garments and cast lots.

LUKE 23:34

Bearing with one another, and forgiving one another, if anyone has a complaint against another; even as Christ forgave you, so you also must do.

COLOSSIANS 3:13

To the praise of the glory of His grace, by which He made us accepted in the Beloved.

In Him we have redemption through His blood,

the forgiveness of sins, according to the riches of His grace.

EPHESIANS 1:6–7

You have forgiven the iniquity of Your people;
You have covered all their sin.

PSALM 85:2

Therefore, if anyone is in Christ, he is a new creation; old things have passed away; behold, all things have become new.

2 CORINTHIANS 5:17

As far as the east is from the west,
So far has He removed our transgressions
from us.

PSALM 103:12

My little children, these things I write to you, so that you may not sin. And if anyone sins, we have an Advocate with the Father, Jesus Christ the righteous.

1 JOHN 2:1

If we confess our sins, He is faithful and just to forgive us our sins and to cleanse us from all unrighteousness.

1 JOHN 1:9

"For I will be merciful to their unrighteousness, and their sins and their lawless deeds I will remember no more."

HEBREWS 8:12

OBEDIENCE

If you fear the LORD and serve Him and obey His voice, and do not rebel against the commandment of the LORD, then both you and the king who reigns over you will continue following the LORD your God.

1 SAMUEL 12:14

So Samuel said:

"Has the LORD as great delight in burnt
offerings and sacrifices,
As in obeying the voice of the LORD?
Behold, to obey is better than sacrifice,
And to heed than the fat of rams.

1 SAMUEL 15:22

"If you are willing and obedient,
You shall eat the good of the land."

ISAIAH 1:19

All we like sheep have gone astray;
We have turned, every one, to his own way;
And the Lord has laid on Him the iniquity of
us all.

ISAIAH 53:6

"Not everyone who says to Me, 'Lord, Lord,' shall enter the kingdom of heaven, but he who does the will of My Father in heaven."

MATTHEW 7:21

Jesus said to them, "My food is to do the will of Him who sent Me, and to finish His work."

JOHN 4:34

And Jesus said to them, "I am the bread of life. He who comes to Me shall never hunger, and he who believes in Me shall never thirst. . . . For I have come down from heaven, not to do My own will, but the will of Him who sent Me."

JOHN 6:35, 38

"If you keep My commandments, you will abide in My love, just as I have kept My Father's commandments and abide in His love."

JOHN 15:10

"Go, stand in the temple and speak to the people all the words of this life." . . . And we are His witnesses to these things, and so also is the Holy Spirit whom God has given to those who obey Him."

ACTS 5:20, 32

For as by one man's disobedience many were made sinners, so also by one Man's obedience many will be made righteous.

ROMANS 5:19

Though He was a Son, yet He learned obedience by the things which He suffered. . . . then He said, "Behold, I have come to do Your will, O God." He takes away the first that He may establish the second."

HEBREWS 5:8; 10:9

By faith Noah, being divinely warned of things not yet seen, moved with godly fear, prepared an ark for the saving of his household, by which he condemned the world and became heir of the righteousness which is according to faith.

By faith Abraham obeyed when he was called to go out to the place which he would receive as an inheritance. And he went out, not knowing where he was going.

HEBREWS 11:7–8

And whatever we ask we receive from Him, because we keep His commandments and do those things that are pleasing in His sight.

1 JOHN 3:22

Now we know that God does not hear sinners; but if anyone is a worshiper of God and does His will, He hears him.

JOHN 9:31

SINCERITY

But from there you will seek the LORD your God, and you will find Him if you seek Him with all your heart and with all your soul.

DEUTERONOMY 4:29

Hear a just cause, O LORD,
Attend to my cry;
Give ear to my prayer which is not from
    deceitful lips.
Let my vindication come from Your presence;
Let Your eyes look on the things that are
    upright.

PSALM 17:1–2

And you will seek Me and find Me, when you search for Me with all your heart.

JEREMIAH 29:13

"But the hour is coming, and now is, when the true worshipers will worship the Father in spirit and truth; for the Father is seeking such to worship Him."

JOHN 4:23

Therefore let us keep the feast, not with old leaven, nor with the leaven of malice and wickedness, but with the unleavened bread of sincerity and truth.

1 CORINTHIANS 5:8

And this I pray, that your love may abound still more and more in knowledge and all discernment, that you may approve the things that are excellent, that you may be sincere and without offense till the day of Christ.

PHILIPPIANS 1:9–10

HUMILITY

Now, O LORD my God, You have made Your servant king instead of my father David, but I am a little child; I do not know how to go out or come in.

1 KINGS 3:7

"If My people who are called by My name will humble themselves, and pray and seek My face, and turn from their wicked ways, then I will hear from heaven, and will forgive their sin and heal their land."

2 CHRONICLES 7:14

LORD, You have heard the desire of the humble;
You will prepare their heart;
You will cause Your ear to hear.

PSALM 10:17

For thus says the High and Lofty One
Who inhabits eternity, whose name is Holy:

"I dwell in the high and holy place,
With him who has a contrite and humble spirit,
To revive the spirit of the humble,
And to revive the heart of the contrite ones."

ISAIAH 57:15

The centurion answered and said, "Lord, I am not worthy that You should come under my roof. But only speak a word, and my servant will be healed."

MATTHEW 8:8

Humble yourselves in the sight of the Lord, and He will lift you up.

JAMES 4:10

PURITY

You shall call, and I will answer You;
You shall desire the work of Your hands.
For now You number my steps,
But do not watch over my sin.
My transgression is sealed up in a bag,
And You cover my iniquity.

JOB 14:15–17

I cried to the LORD with my voice,
And He heard me from His holy hill.

PSALM 3:4

Lead me, O LORD, in Your righteousness
        because of my enemies;
Make Your way straight before my face.

PSALM 5:8

Keep back Your servant also from
        presumptuous sins;
Let them not have dominion over me.
Then I shall be blameless,
And I shall be innocent of great transgression.

Let the words of my mouth and the meditation
        of my heart
Be acceptable in Your sight,
O LORD, my strength and my Redeemer.

PSALM 19:13–14

The earth is the LORD's, and all its fullness,
The world and those who dwell therein.
For He has founded it upon the seas,
And established it upon the waters.

Who may ascend into the hill of the Lord?
Or who may stand in His holy place?
He who has clean hands and a pure heart,
Who has not lifted up his soul to an idol,
Nor sworn deceitfully.
He shall receive blessing from the Lord,
And righteousness from the God of his
        salvation.
This is Jacob, the generation of those who
        seek Him,
Who seek Your face.

PSALM 24:1–6

Vindicate me, O Lord,
For I have walked in my integrity.
I have also trusted in the Lord;
I shall not slip.
Examine me, O Lord, and prove me;
Try my mind and my heart.

PSALM 26:1–2

Create in me a clean heart, O God,
And renew a steadfast spirit within me.

PSALM 51:10

If I regard iniquity in my heart,
The Lord will not hear.
But certainly God has heard me;
He has attended to the voice of my prayer.

PSALM 66:18–19

Search me, O God, and know my heart;
Try me, and know my anxieties;
And see if there is any wicked way in me,
And lead me in the way everlasting.

PSALM 139:23–24

But He hears the prayer of the righteous.

PROVERBS 15:29

So I said:

"Woe is me, for I am undone!
Because I am a man of unclean lips,
And I dwell in the midst of a people of
        unclean lips;
For my eyes have seen the King,
The Lord of hosts."

ISAIAH 6:5

But let man and beast be covered with sackcloth, and cry mightily to God; yes, let every one turn from his evil way and from the violence that is in his hands.

JONAH 3:8

To grant us that we,
Being delivered from the hand of our enemies,
Might serve Him without fear,
In holiness and righteousness before Him all
    the days of our life.

LUKE 1:74–75

Therefore, having these promises, beloved, let us cleanse ourselves from all filthiness of the flesh and spirit, perfecting holiness in the fear of God.

2 CORINTHIANS 7:1

"For the eyes of the LORD are on the righteous,
And His ears are open to their prayers;
But the face of the LORD is against those who
    do evil."

1 PETER 3:12

The LORD is far from the wicked,
But He hears the prayer of the righteous.

PROVERBS 15:29

JOY

But rejoice to the extent that you partake of Christ's
sufferings, that when His glory is revealed, you may
also be glad with exceeding joy.

1 PETER 4:13

Now to Him who is able to keep you from
stumbling,
And to present you faultless
Before the presence of His glory with
exceeding joy.

JUDE 24

The king shall have joy in Your strength,
O LORD;
And in Your salvation how greatly shall he
rejoice!
You have given him his heart's desire,
And have not withheld the request of his lips.

PSALM 21:1–2

And my soul shall be joyful in the LORD;
It shall rejoice in His salvation.

PSALM 35:9

Let them shout for joy and be glad,
Who favor my righteous cause;
And let them say continually,
"Let the LORD be magnified,
Who has pleasure in the prosperity of His
      servant."
And my tongue shall speak of Your
      righteousness
And of Your praise all the day long.

PSALM 35:27–28

Create in me a clean heart, O God,
And renew a steadfast spirit within me.
Do not cast me away from Your presence,
And do not take Your Holy Spirit from me.

Restore to me the joy of Your salvation,
And uphold me by Your generous Spirit.
Then I will teach transgressors Your ways,
And sinners shall be converted to You.

PSALM 51:10–13

CONDITIONS OF PRAYER

John 15:7 says, "If you abide in Me, and My words abide in you, you will ask what you desire, and it shall be done for you." The conditions of prayer are simple. Abide with and spend time with the Lord in prayer, and let the words of Scripture become a part of us, to obey and live in His presence. Our prayers will then have meaning because God will be listening, and His Spirit will guide us as we seek to be obedient to His Word and live a life that is pleasing to the Father.

PRAYING IN THE WORD

My son, give attention to my words;
> Incline your ear to my sayings.
> Do not let them depart from your eyes;
> Keep them in the midst of your heart;
> For they are life to those who find them,
> And health to all their flesh.
> Keep your heart with all diligence,

For out of it spring the issues of life.

PROVERBS 4:20–23

Your words were found, and I ate them,
And Your word was to me the joy and rejoicing
     of my heart;
For I am called by Your name,
O Lord God of hosts.

JEREMIAH 15:16

The centurion answered and said, "Lord, I am not worthy that You should come under my roof. But only speak a word, and my servant will be healed."

MATTHEW 8:8

"If you abide in Me, and My words abide in you, you will ask what you desire, and it shall be done for you."

JOHN 15:7

"And for their sakes I sanctify Myself, that they also may be sanctified by the truth.

"I do not pray for these alone, but also for those who will believe in Me through their word."

JOHN 17:19–20

But we will give ourselves continually to prayer and to the ministry of the word.

ACTS 6:4

Finally, brethren, pray for us, that the word of the Lord may run swiftly and be glorified, just as it is with you.

2 THESSALONIANS 3:1

For every creature of God is good, and nothing is to be refused if it is received with thanksgiving; for it is sanctified by the word of God and prayer.

1 TIMOTHY 4:4–5

"If anyone wills to do His will, he shall know concerning the doctrine, whether it is from God or whether I speak on My own authority."

JOHN 7:17

And they prayed and said, "You, O Lord, who know the hearts of all, show which of these two You have chosen."

ACTS 1:24

So when he would not be persuaded, we ceased, saying, "The will of the Lord be done."

ACTS 21:14

And do not be conformed to this world, but be transformed by the renewing of your mind, that you may prove what is that good and acceptable and perfect will of God.

ROMANS 12:2

Therefore do not be unwise, but understand what the will of the Lord is.

EPHESIANS 5:17

For this reason we also, since the day we heard it, do not cease to pray for you, and to ask that you may be filled with the knowledge of His will in all wisdom and spiritual understanding.

COLOSSIANS 1:9

Now this is the confidence that we have in Him, that if we ask anything according to His will, He hears us.

1 JOHN 5:14

And He was preaching in their synagogues throughout all Galilee, and casting out demons.

Now a leper came to Him, imploring Him, kneeling down to Him and saying to Him, "If You are willing, You can make me clean."

Then Jesus, moved with compassion, stretched out His hand and touched him, and said to him, "I am willing; be cleansed." As soon as He had spoken, immediately the leprosy left him, and he was cleansed.

MARK 1:39–42

Jesus said to them, "My food is to do the will of Him who sent Me, and to finish His work."

JOHN 4:34

PRAYING IN FAITH

Now faith is the substance of things hoped for, the evidence of things not seen. For by it the elders obtained a good testimony.

By faith we understand that the worlds were framed by the word of God, so that the things which are seen were not made of things which are visible.

By faith Abel offered to God a more excellent

sacrifice than Cain, through which he obtained witness that he was righteous, God testifying of his gifts; and through it he being dead still speaks.

By faith Enoch was taken away so that he did not see death, "and was not found, because God had taken him"; for before he was taken he had this testimony, that he pleased God. But without faith it is impossible to please Him, for he who comes to God must believe that He is, and that He is a rewarder of those who diligently seek Him.

By faith Noah, being divinely warned of things not yet seen, moved with godly fear, prepared an ark for the saving of his household, by which he condemned the world and became heir of the righteousness which is according to faith.

By faith Abraham obeyed when he was called to go out to the place which he would receive as an inheritance. And he went out, not knowing where he was going. By faith he dwelt in the land of promise as in a foreign country, dwelling in tents with Isaac and Jacob, the heirs with him of the same promise; for he waited for the city which has foundations, whose builder and maker is God.

By faith Sarah herself also received strength to conceive seed, and she bore a child when she was past the age, because she judged Him faithful who had promised. Therefore from one man, and him as good as dead, were born as many as the stars of the sky in multitude—innumerable as the sand which is by the seashore.

These all died in faith, not having received the promises, but having seen them afar off were assured of them, embraced them and confessed that they were strangers and pilgrims on the earth. For those who say such things declare plainly that they seek a homeland. And truly if they had called to mind that country from which they had come out, they would have had opportunity to return. But now they desire a better, that is, a heavenly country. Therefore God is not ashamed to be called their God, for He has prepared a city for them.

By faith Abraham, when he was tested, offered up Isaac, and he who had received the promises offered up his only begotten son, of whom it was said, "In Isaac your seed shall be called," concluding that God was able to raise him up, even from the dead, from which he also received him in a figurative sense.

By faith Isaac blessed Jacob and Esau concerning things to come.

By faith Jacob, when he was dying, blessed each

of the sons of Joseph, and worshiped, leaning on the top of his staff.

By faith Joseph, when he was dying, made mention of the departure of the children of Israel, and gave instructions concerning his bones.

By faith Moses, when he was born, was hidden three months by his parents, because they saw he was a beautiful child; and they were not afraid of the king's command.

By faith Moses, when he became of age, refused to be called the son of Pharaoh's daughter, choosing rather to suffer affliction with the people of God than to enjoy the passing pleasures of sin, esteeming the reproach of Christ greater riches than the treasures in Egypt; for he looked to the reward.

By faith he forsook Egypt, not fearing the wrath of the king; for he endured as seeing Him who is invisible. By faith he kept the Passover and the sprinkling of blood, lest he who destroyed the first-born should touch them.

By faith they passed through the Red Sea as by dry land, whereas the Egyptians, attempting to do so, were drowned.

By faith the walls of Jericho fell down after they were encircled for seven days. By faith the harlot

Rahab did not perish with those who did not believe, when she had received the spies with peace.

And what more shall I say? For the time would fail me to tell of Gideon and Barak and Samson and Jephthah, also of David and Samuel and the prophets: who through faith subdued kingdoms, worked righteousness, obtained promises, stopped the mouths of lions, quenched the violence of fire, escaped the edge of the sword, out of weakness were made strong, became valiant in battle, turned to flight the armies of the aliens. Women received their dead raised to life again.

Others were tortured, not accepting deliverance, that they might obtain a better resurrection. Still others had trial of mockings and scourgings, yes, and of chains and imprisonment. They were stoned, they were sawn in two, were tempted, were slain with the sword. They wandered about in sheepskins and goatskins, being destitute, afflicted, tormented—of whom the world was not worthy. They wandered in deserts and mountains, in dens and caves of the earth.

And all these, having obtained a good testimony through faith, did not receive the promise, God having provided something better for us, that they should not be made perfect apart from us.

HEBREWS 11:1–40

And when they had come to the multitude, a man came to Him, kneeling down to Him and saying, "Lord, have mercy on my son, for he is an epileptic and suffers severely; for he often falls into the fire and often into the water. So I brought him to Your disciples, but they could not cure him."

Then Jesus answered and said, "O faithless and perverse generation, how long shall I be with you? How long shall I bear with you? Bring him here to Me." And Jesus rebuked the demon, and it came out of him; and the child was cured from that very hour.

Then the disciples came to Jesus privately and said, "Why could we not cast it out?"

So Jesus said to them, "Because of your unbelief; for assuredly, I say to you, if you have faith as a mustard seed, you will say to this mountain, 'Move from here to there,' and it will move; and nothing will be impossible for you."

MATTHEW 17:14–20

Now in the morning, as He returned to the city, He was hungry. And seeing a fig tree by the road, He came to it and found nothing on it but leaves, and said to it, "Let no fruit grow on you ever again." Immediately the fig tree withered away.

And when the disciples saw it, they marveled, saying, "How did the fig tree wither away so soon?"

So Jesus answered and said to them, "Assuredly, I say to you, if you have faith and do not doubt, you will not only do what was done to the fig tree, but also if you say to this mountain, 'Be removed and be cast into the sea,' it will be done."

MATTHEW 21:18–21

If then God so clothes the grass, which today is in the field and tomorrow is thrown into the oven, how much more will He clothe you, O you of little faith?

LUKE 12:28

Through whom also we have access by faith into this grace in which we stand, and rejoice in hope of the glory of God.

ROMANS 5:2

That you do not become sluggish, but imitate those who through faith and patience inherit the promises.

HEBREWS 6:12

And suddenly, a woman who had a flow of blood for twelve years came from behind and touched the hem of His garment. For she said to herself, "If only I may touch His garment, I shall be made well." But Jesus turned around, and when He saw her He said, "Be of good cheer, daughter; your faith has made you well." And the woman was made well from that hour.

When Jesus came into the ruler's house, and saw the flute players and the noisy crowd wailing, He said to them, "Make room, for the girl is not dead, but sleeping." And they ridiculed Him. But when the crowd was put outside, He went in and took her by the hand, and the girl arose. And the report of this went out into all that land.

MATTHEW 9:20–26

And immediately Jesus stretched out His hand and caught him, and said to him, "O you of little faith, why did you doubt?" . . . And they begged Him that they might only touch the hem of His garment. And as many as touched it were made perfectly well.

MATTHEW 14:31, 36

Then Jesus answered and said to her, "O woman, great is your faith! Let it be to you as you desire." And her daughter was healed from that very hour.

MATTHEW 15:28

So Jesus answered and said to them, "Have faith in God. For assuredly, I say to you, whoever says to this mountain, 'Be removed and be cast into the sea,' and does not doubt in his heart, but believes that those things he says will be done, he will have whatever he says. Therefore I say to you, whatever things you ask when you pray, believe that you receive them, and you will have them."

MARK 11:22–24

And the apostles said to the Lord, "Increase our faith."

LUKE 17:5

For in it the righteousness of God is revealed from faith to faith; as it is written, "The just shall live by faith."

ROMANS 1:17

He did not waver at the promise of God through unbelief, but was strengthened in faith, giving glory to God, and being fully convinced that what He had promised He was also able to perform.

ROMANS 4:20–21

So then faith comes by hearing, and hearing by the word of God.

ROMANS 10:17

But he who doubts is condemned if he eats, because he does not eat from faith; for whatever is not from faith is sin.

ROMANS 14:23

While we do not look at the things which are seen, but at the things which are not seen. For the things which are seen are temporary, but the things which are not seen are eternal.

2 CORINTHIANS 4:18

For in Christ Jesus neither circumcision nor uncircumcision avails anything, but faith working through love.

GALATIANS 5:6

For this reason we also thank God without ceasing, because when you received the word of God which you heard from us, you welcomed it not as the word of men, but as it is in truth, the word of God, which also effectively works in you who believe.

1 THESSALONIANS 2:13

But let him ask in faith, with no doubting, for he who doubts is like a wave of the sea driven and tossed by the wind. For let not that man suppose that he will receive anything from the Lord.

JAMES 1:6–7

And the prayer of faith will save the sick, and the Lord will raise him up. And if he has committed sins, he will be forgiven.

JAMES 5:15

For whatever is born of God overcomes the world. And this is the victory that has overcome the world—our faith.

1 JOHN 5:4

Through whom also we have access by faith into this grace in which we stand, and rejoice in hope of the glory of God.

ROMANS 5:2

For through Him we both have access by one Spirit to the Father.

EPHESIANS 2:18

Which in other ages was not made known to the sons of men, as it has now been revealed by the Spirit to His holy apostles and prophets: that the Gentiles should be fellow heirs, of the same body, and partakers of His promise in Christ through the gospel, of which I became a minister according to the gift of the grace of God given to me by the effective working of His power.

To me, who am less than the least of all the saints, this grace was given, that I should preach among the Gentiles the unsearchable riches of Christ, and to make all see what is the fellowship of the mystery, which from the beginning of the ages has been hidden in God who created all things through Jesus Christ; to the intent that now the manifold wisdom of God might be made known by the church to the principalities and powers in the heavenly places, according to the eternal purpose which He accomplished in Christ Jesus our Lord, in whom we have boldness and access with confidence through faith in Him.

EPHESIANS 3:5–12

Therefore, brethren, having boldness to enter the Holiest by the blood of Jesus, by a new and living way which He consecrated for us, through the veil, that is, His flesh, and having a High Priest over the house of God, let us draw near with a true heart in full assurance of faith, having our hearts sprinkled from an evil conscience and our bodies washed with pure water. Let us hold fast the confession of our hope without wavering, for He who promised is faithful.

HEBREWS 10:19–23

PRAYING IN THE SPIRIT

For if I pray in a tongue, my spirit prays, but my understanding is unfruitful. What is the conclusion then? I will pray with the spirit, and I will also pray with the understanding. I will sing with the spirit, and I will also sing with the understanding.

1 CORINTHIANS 14:14–15

Praying always with all prayer and supplication in the Spirit, being watchful to this end with all perseverance and supplication for all the saints.

EPHESIANS 6:18

But you, beloved, building yourselves up on your most holy faith, praying in the Holy Spirit, keep yourselves in the love of God, looking for the mercy of our Lord Jesus Christ unto eternal life.

JUDE 1:20–21

However, when He, the Spirit of truth, has come, He will guide you into all truth; for He will not speak on His own authority, but whatever He hears He will speak; and He will tell you things to come.

JOHN 16:13

Likewise the Spirit also helps in our weaknesses. For we do not know what we should pray for as we ought, but the Spirit Himself makes intercession for us with groanings which cannot be uttered. Now He who searches the hearts knows what the mind of the Spirit is, because He makes intercession for the saints according to the will of God.

ROMANS 8:26–27

HINDERANCES TO PRAYER

"Then you answered and said to me, 'We have sinned against the LORD; we will go up and fight, just as the

LORD our God commanded us.' And when everyone of you had girded on his weapons of war, you were ready to go up into the mountain.

"And the LORD said to me, 'Tell them, "Do not go up nor fight, for I am not among you; lest you be defeated before your enemies."' So I spoke to you; yet you would not listen, but rebelled against the command of the LORD, and presumptuously went up into the mountain. And the Amorites who dwelt in that mountain came out against you and chased you as bees do, and drove you back from Seir to Hormah. Then you returned and wept before the LORD, but the LORD would not listen to your voice nor give ear to you."

DEUTERONOMY 1:41–45

"But the LORD was angry with me on your account, and would not listen to me. So the LORD said to me: 'Enough of that! Speak no more to Me of this matter.'"

DEUTERONOMY 3:26

Then Joshua tore his clothes, and fell to the earth on his face before the ark of the LORD until evening, he and the elders of Israel; and they put dust on their heads. And Joshua said, "Alas, Lord GOD, why have

You brought this people over the Jordan at all—to deliver us into the hand of the Amorites, to destroy us? Oh, that we had been content, and dwelt on the other side of the Jordan! O Lord, what shall I say when Israel turns its back before its enemies? For the Canaanites and all the inhabitants of the land will hear it, and surround us, and cut off our name from the earth. Then what will You do for Your great name?"

JOSHUA 7:6-9

There they cry out, but He does not answer,
Because of the pride of evil men.
Surely God will not listen to empty talk,
Nor will the Almighty regard it.

JOB 35:12-13

If I regard iniquity in my heart,
The Lord will not hear.

PSALM 66:18

Because I have called and you refused,
I have stretched out my hand and no one
        regarded,
Because you disdained all my counsel,

And would have none of my rebuke,
I also will laugh at your calamity;
I will mock when your terror comes,
When your terror comes like a storm,
And your destruction comes like a whirlwind,
When distress and anguish come upon you.

"Then they will call on me, but I will not
answer;
They will seek me diligently, but they will not
find me.
Because they hated knowledge
And did not choose the fear of the LORD,
They would have none of my counsel
And despised my every rebuke.

PROVERBS 1:24–30

The sacrifice of the wicked is an abomination to
the LORD,
But the prayer of the upright is His delight.

PROVERBS 15:8

Whoever shuts his ears to the cry of the poor
Will also cry himself and not be heard.

PROVERBS 21:13

One who turns away his ear from hearing
    the law,
Even his prayer is an abomination.

PROVERBS 28:9

"When you spread out your hands,
I will hide My eyes from you;
Even though you make many prayers,
I will not hear.
Your hands are full of blood."

ISAIAH 1:15

Behold, the LORD's hand is not shortened,
That it cannot save;
Nor His ear heavy,
That it cannot hear.
But your iniquities have separated you from
    your God;
And your sins have hidden His face from you,
So that He will not hear.

ISAIAH 59:1–2

Therefore thus says the LORD: "Behold, I will surely
bring calamity on them which they will not be able

to escape; and though they cry out to Me, I will not listen to them."

JEREMIAH 11:11

Then the LORD said to me, "Even if Moses and Samuel stood before Me, My mind would not be favorable toward this people. Cast them out of My sight, and let them go forth."

JEREMIAH 15:1

Even when I cry and shout,
He shuts out my prayer. . . .

You have covered Yourself with a cloud,
That prayer should not pass through.

LAMENTATIONS 3:8, 44

Now some of the elders of Israel came to me and sat before me. And the word of the LORD came to me, saying, "Son of man, these men have set up their idols in their hearts, and put before them that which causes them to stumble into iniquity. Should I let Myself be inquired of at all by them?"

EZEKIEL 14:1–3

Then they will cry to the LORD,
But He will not hear them;
He will even hide His face from them at
        that time,
Because they have been evil in their deeds.

MICAH 3:4

"But they refused to heed, shrugged their shoulders, and stopped their ears so that they could not hear. Yes, they made their hearts like flint, refusing to hear the law and the words which the LORD of hosts had sent by His Spirit through the former prophets. Thus great wrath came from the LORD of hosts. Therefore it happened, that just as He proclaimed and they would not hear, so they called out and I would not listen," says the LORD of hosts.

ZECHARIAH 7:11–13

"With their flocks and herds
They shall go to seek the LORD,
But they will not find Him;
He has withdrawn Himself from them.

HOSEA 5:6

Now I pray to God that you do no evil, not that we should appear approved, but that you should do what is honorable, though we may seem disqualified.

2 CORINTHIANS 13:7

You lust and do not have. You murder and covet and cannot obtain. You fight and war. Yet you do not have because you do not ask. You ask and do not receive, because you ask amiss, that you may spend it on your pleasures.

JAMES 4:2–3

Husbands, likewise, dwell with them with understanding, giving honor to the wife, as to the weaker vessel, and as being heirs together of the grace of life, that your prayers may not be hindered. . . .

"For the eyes of the LORD are on the righteous,
And His ears are open to their prayers;
But the face of the LORD is against those who
do evil."

1 PETER 3:7, 12

SPIRITUAL WARFARE THROUGH PRAYER

We have an advocate, the heavenly Father, whom we join hands with when we come to Him in prayer. First John 5:14 says, "Now this is the confidence that we have in Him, that if we ask anything according to His will, He hears us." The Lord stands ready to help us, defend us, and go before us as we face various obstacles in our lives. Jesus is our partner, and He wants the best for us. When we fight all of our battles on our knees, we will win every time.

AUTHORITY IN THE NAME OF JESUS

Let the word of Christ dwell in you richly in all wisdom, teaching and admonishing one another in psalms and hymns and spiritual songs, singing with grace in your hearts to the Lord. And whatever you do in word or deed, do all in the name of the Lord Jesus, giving thanks to God the Father through Him.

COLOSSIANS 3:16–17

"And in that day you will ask Me nothing. Most assuredly, I say to you, whatever you ask the Father in My name He will give you. Until now you have asked nothing in My name. Ask, and you will receive, that your joy may be full."

JOHN 16:23–24

"If you abide in Me, and My words abide in you, you will ask what you desire, and it shall be done for you. By this My Father is glorified, that you bear much fruit; so you will be My disciples.

"As the Father loved Me, I also have loved you; abide in My love. If you keep My commandments, you will abide in My love, just as I have kept My Father's commandments and abide in His love. . . .

"You did not choose Me, but I chose you and appointed you that you should go and bear fruit, and that your fruit should remain, that whatever you ask the Father in My name He may give you."

JOHN 15:7–10, 16

For if our heart condemns us, God is greater than our heart, and knows all things. Beloved, if our heart does not condemn us, we have confidence toward God. And whatever we ask we receive from Him, because we keep His commandments and do those things that are pleasing in His sight.

1 JOHN 3:20–22

Now this is the confidence that we have in Him, that if we ask anything according to His will, He hears us. And if we know that He hears us, whatever we ask, we know that we have the petitions that we have asked of Him.

1 JOHN 5:14–15

So Jesus said to them, "Because of your unbelief; for assuredly, I say to you, if you have faith as a mustard seed, you will say to this mountain, 'Move from here to there,' and it will move; and nothing will be impossible for you. However, this kind does not go out except by prayer and fasting."

Now while they were staying in Galilee, Jesus said to them, "The Son of Man is about to be betrayed into the hands of men, and they will kill Him, and the third day He will be raised up." And they were exceedingly sorrowful.

MATTHEW 17:20–23

"I will bring the one-third through the fire,
Will refine them as silver is refined,
And test them as gold is tested.
They will call on My name,
And I will answer them.
I will say, 'This is My people';
And each one will say, 'The LORD is my God.'"

ZECHARIAH 13:9

"Again I say to you that if two of you agree on earth concerning anything that they ask, it will be done for them by My Father in heaven. For where two or three are gathered together in My name, I am there in the midst of them."

MATTHEW 18:19–20

"And these signs will follow those who believe: In My name they will cast out demons; they will speak with new tongues."

MARK 16:17

"Most assuredly, I say to you, he who believes in Me, the works that I do he will do also; and greater works than these he will do, because I go to My Father. And whatever you ask in My name, that I will do, that the

Father may be glorified in the Son. If you ask anything in My name, I will do it."

PERSISTENCE AND PREVAILING IN PRAYER

Then Jacob was left alone; and a Man wrestled with him until the breaking of day. Now when He saw that He did not prevail against him, He touched the socket of his hip; and the socket of Jacob's hip was out of joint as He wrestled with him. And He said, "Let Me go, for the day breaks."

But he said, "I will not let You go unless You bless me!"

Blessed be the LORD my Rock,
Who trains my hands for war,
And my fingers for battle.

Put on the whole armor of God, that you may be able to stand against the wiles of the devil. For we do not wrestle against flesh and blood, but against principalities, against powers, against the rulers of the darkness of this age, against spiritual hosts of wickedness in the heavenly places.

EPHESIANS 6:11–12

So Ahab went up to eat and drink. And Elijah went up to the top of Carmel; then he bowed down on the ground, and put his face between his knees, and said to his servant, "Go up now, look toward the sea."

So he went up and looked, and said, "There is nothing." And seven times he said, "Go again."

Then it came to pass the seventh time, that he said, "There is a cloud, as small as a man's hand, rising out of the sea!" So he said, "Go up, say to Ahab, 'Prepare your chariot, and go down before the rain stops you.'"

Now it happened in the meantime that the sky became black with clouds and wind, and there was a heavy rain. So Ahab rode away and went to Jezreel.

1 KINGS 18:42–45

Seek the LORD and His strength;
Seek His face evermore!

1 CHRONICLES 16:11

And behold, a woman of Canaan came from that region and cried out to Him, saying, "Have mercy on me, O Lord, Son of David! My daughter is severely demon-possessed."

But He answered her not a word.

And His disciples came and urged Him, saying, "Send her away, for she cries out after us."

But He answered and said, "I was not sent except to the lost sheep of the house of Israel."

Then she came and worshiped Him, saying, "Lord, help me!"

But He answered and said, "It is not good to take the children's bread and throw it to the little dogs."

And she said, "Yes, Lord, yet even the little dogs eat the crumbs which fall from their masters' table."

Then Jesus answered and said to her, "O woman, great is your faith! Let it be to you as you desire." And her daughter was healed from that very hour.

MATTHEW 15:22–28

Now it came to pass in those days that He went out to the mountain to pray, and continued all night in prayer to God.

LUKE 6:12

And He said to them, "Which of you shall have a friend, and go to him at midnight and say to him, 'Friend, lend me three loaves; for a friend of mine has come to me on his journey, and I have nothing to set before him'; and he will answer from within and say, 'Do not trouble me; the door is now shut, and my children are with me in bed; I cannot rise and give to you'? I say to you, though he will not rise and give to him because he is his friend, yet because of his persistence he will rise and give him as many as he needs.

"So I say to you, ask, and it will be given to you; seek, and you will find; knock, and it will be opened to you. For everyone who asks receives, and he who seeks finds, and to him who knocks it will be opened."

LUKE 11:5–10

Then He spoke a parable to them, that men always ought to pray and not lose heart, saying: "There was in a certain city a judge who did not fear God nor regard man. Now there was a widow in that city; and she came to him, saying, 'Get justice for me from my adversary.' And he would not for a while; but afterward he said within himself, 'Though I do not fear God nor regard man, yet because this widow troubles me I will avenge her, lest by her continual coming she weary me.'"

Then the Lord said, "Hear what the unjust judge said. And shall God not avenge His own elect who cry out day and night to Him, though He bears long with them?"

LUKE 18:1–7

And being in agony, He prayed more earnestly. Then His sweat became like great drops of blood falling down to the ground.

LUKE 22:44

These all continued with one accord in prayer and supplication, with the women and Mary the mother of Jesus, and with His brothers.

ACTS 1:14

Then those who gladly received his word were baptized; and that day about three thousand souls were added to them. And they continued steadfastly in the apostles' doctrine and fellowship, in the breaking of bread, and in prayers.

ACTS 2:41–42

Praying always with all prayer and supplication in the Spirit, being watchful to this end with all perseverance and supplication for all the saints—and for me, that utterance may be given to me, that I may open my mouth boldly to make known the mystery of the gospel, for which I am an ambassador in chains; that in it I may speak boldly, as I ought to speak.

EPHESIANS 6:18–20

Continue earnestly in prayer, being vigilant in it with thanksgiving; meanwhile praying also for us, that God would open to us a door for the word, to speak the mystery of Christ, for which I am also in chains.

COLOSSIANS 4:2–3

My friends scorn me;
My eyes pour out tears to God.

JOB 16:20

I am weary with my groaning;
All night I make my bed swim;
I drench my couch with my tears.

PSALM 6:6

For His anger is but for a moment,
His favor is for life;
Weeping may endure for a night,
But joy comes in the morning.

PSALM 30:5

You number my wanderings;
Put my tears into Your bottle;
Are they not in Your book?
When I cry out to You,
Then my enemies will turn back;
This I know, because God is for me.
In God (I will praise His word),
In the Lord (I will praise His word),
In God I have put my trust;
I will not be afraid.
What can man do to me?

Vows made to You are binding upon me, O God;
I will render praises to You,
For You have delivered my soul from death.
Have You not kept my feet from falling,
That I may walk before God
In the light of the living?

PSALM 56:8–20

Those who sow in tears
Shall reap in joy.

PSALM 126:5

Oh, that my head were waters,
And my eyes a fountain of tears,
That I might weep day and night
For the slain of the daughter of my people!

JEREMIAH 9:1

Jesus said to him, "If you can believe, all things are possible to him who believes."

Immediately the father of the child cried out and said with tears, "Lord, I believe; help my unbelief!"

MARK 9:23–24

"Blessed are you who hunger now,
For you shall be filled.
Blessed are you who weep now,
For you shall laugh."

LUKE 6:21

At Joppa there was a certain disciple named Tabitha, which is translated Dorcas. This woman was full of good works and charitable deeds which she did. But it happened in those days that she became sick and died. When they had washed her, they laid her in an upper room. And since Lydda was near Joppa, and the disciples had heard that Peter was there, they sent two men to him, imploring him not to delay in coming to them. Then Peter arose and went with them. When he had come, they brought him to the upper room. And all the widows stood by him weeping, showing the tunics and garments which Dorcas had made while she was with them.

ACTS 9:36–39

Let integrity and uprightness preserve me,
For I wait for You.

PSALM 25:21

Wait on the LORD;
Be of good courage,
And He shall strengthen your heart;
Wait, I say, on the LORD!

PSALM 27:14

I waited patiently for the LORD;
And He inclined to me,

And heard my cry.

PSALM 40:1

I wait for the LORD, my soul waits,
And in His word I do hope.

PSALM 130:5

But those who wait on the LORD
Shall renew their strength;
They shall mount up with wings like eagles,
They shall run and not be weary,
They shall walk and not faint.

ISAIAH 40:31

Therefore I will look to the LORD;
I will wait for the God of my salvation;
My God will hear me.

MICAH 7:7

Nevertheless we made our prayer to our God, and because of them we set a watch against them day and night.

NEHEMIAH 4:9

"Watch and pray, lest you enter into temptation. The spirit indeed is willing, but the flesh is weak."

MATTHEW 26:41

"Watch therefore, and pray always that you may be counted worthy to escape all these things that will come to pass, and to stand before the Son of Man."

LUKE 21:36

Continue earnestly in prayer, being vigilant in it with thanksgiving.

COLOSSIANS 4:2

But the end of all things is at hand; therefore be serious and watchful in your prayers.

1 PETER 4:7

And there is no one who calls on Your name,
Who stirs himself up to take hold of You;
For You have hidden Your face from us,
And have consumed us because of our
    iniquities.

ISAIAH 64:7

"And when you pray, you shall not be like the hypocrites. For they love to pray standing in the synagogues and on the corners of the streets, that they may be seen by men. Assuredly, I say to you, they have their reward. But you, when you pray, go into your room, and when you have shut your door, pray to your Father who is in the secret place; and your Father who sees in secret will reward you openly. And when you pray, do not use vain repetitions as the heathen do. For they think that they will be heard for their many words.

"Therefore do not be like them. For your Father knows the things you have need of before you ask Him."

MATTHEW 6:5–8

So Jesus answered and said to them, "Assuredly, I say to you, if you have faith and do not doubt, you will not only do what was done to the fig tree, but also if you say to this mountain, 'Be removed and be cast into the sea,' it will be done. And whatever things you ask in prayer, believing, you will receive."

MATTHEW 21:21–22

"Therefore I say to you, whatever things you ask when you pray, believe that you receive them, and you will have them."

MARK 11:24

Let us therefore come boldly to the throne of grace, that we may obtain mercy and find grace to help in time of need.

HEBREWS 4:16

PETITIONS AND PATTERNS FOR PRAYER

Then He spoke a parable to them, that men always ought to pray and not lose heart.

LUKE 18:1

For this reason we also, since the day we heard it, do not cease to pray for you, and to ask that you may be filled with the knowledge of His will in all wisdom and spiritual understanding.

COLOSSIANS 1:9

So, affectionately longing for you, we were well pleased to impart to you not only the gospel of God, but also our own lives, because you had become dear to us.

1 THESSALONIANS 2:8

Pray without ceasing, in everything give thanks; for this is the will of God in Christ Jesus for you.

1 THESSALONIANS 5:17–18

Therefore we also pray always for you that our God would count you worthy of this calling, and fulfill all the good pleasure of His goodness and the work of faith with power.

2 THESSALONIANS 1:11

I cried out to You, O Lord;
And to the Lord I made supplication

PSALM 30:8

Evening and morning and at noon
I will pray, and cry aloud,
And He shall hear my voice.

PSALM 55:17

So Moses went out of the city from Pharaoh and spread out his hands to the Lord; then the thunder

and the hail ceased, and the rain was not poured on
the earth.

EXODUS 9:33

So the Lord said to Moses, "I will also do this thing
that you have spoken; for you have found grace in My
sight, and I know you by name."

EXODUS 33:17

"Then I pleaded with the LORD at that time, saying:
'O Lord GOD, You have begun to show Your servant
Your greatness and Your mighty hand, for what god is
there in heaven or on earth who can do anything like
Your works and Your mighty deeds?'"

DEUTERONOMY 3:23–24

In God (I will praise His word),
In God I have put my trust;
I will not fear.
What can flesh do to me?

PSALM 56:4

Remember me, O LORD, with the favor You
have toward Your people.

Oh, visit me with Your salvation,
That I may see the benefit of Your chosen ones,
That I may rejoice in the gladness of Your
      nation,
That I may glory with Your inheritance.

PSALM 106:4–5

I will offer to You the sacrifice of thanksgiving,
And will call upon the name of the LORD.

PSALM 116:17

"Ask, and it will be given to you; seek, and you will find; knock, and it will be opened to you. For everyone who asks receives, and he who seeks finds, and to him who knocks it will be opened. Or what man is there among you who, if his son asks for bread, will give him a stone? Or if he asks for a fish, will he give him a serpent? If you then, being evil, know how to give good gifts to your children, how much more will your Father who is in heaven give good things to those who ask Him!"

MATTHEW 7:7–11

Yet regard the prayer of Your servant and his supplication, O LORD my God, and listen to the cry and the prayer which Your servant is praying before You.

2 CHRONICLES 6:19

Only two things do not do to me,
Then I will not hide myself from You:
Withdraw Your hand far from me,
And let not the dread of You make me afraid.
Then call, and I will answer;
Or let me speak, then You respond to me.

JOB 13:20–22

So that they caused the cry of the poor to come
    to Him;
For He hears the cry of the afflicted.

JOB 34:28

But know that the Lord has set apart for
    Himself him who is godly;
The Lord will hear when I call to Him.

PSALM 4:3

Give ear to my words, O Lord,
Consider my meditation.

Give heed to the voice of my cry,
My King and my God,
For to You I will pray.
My voice You shall hear in the morning,
    O Lord;
In the morning I will direct it to You,
And I will look up.

PSALM 5:1–3

The Lord is far from the wicked,
But He hears the prayer of the righteous.

PROVERBS 15:29

Cast your bread upon the waters,
For you will find it after many days.

ECCLESIASTES 11:1

"I will give you the treasures of darkness
And hidden riches of secret places,
That you may know that I, the Lord,
Who call you by your name,
Am the God of Israel."

ISAIAH 45:3

"Then you shall call, and the LORD will answer;
You shall cry, and He will say, 'Here I am.'

"If you take away the yoke from your midst,
The pointing of the finger, and speaking
     wickedness."
ISAIAH 58:9

"Call to Me, and I will answer you, and show you
great and mighty things, which you do not know."
JEREMIAH 33:3

"I will strengthen the house of Judah,
And I will save the house of Joseph.
I will bring them back,
Because I have mercy on them.
They shall be as though I had not cast them
     aside;
For I am the LORD their God,
And I will hear them."
ZECHARIAH 10:6

Then the man bowed down his head and worshiped
the LORD. . . . And I bowed my head and worshiped
the LORD, and blessed the LORD God of my master

Abraham, who had led me in the way of truth to take the daughter of my master's brother for his son. . . . And it came to pass, when Abraham's servant heard their words, that he worshiped the LORD, bowing himself to the earth.

GENESIS 24:26, 48, 52

"And when you pray, you shall not be like the hypocrites. For they love to pray standing in the synagogues and on the corners of the streets, that they may be seen by men. Assuredly, I say to you, they have their reward. But you, when you pray, go into your room, and when you have shut your door, pray to your Father who is in the secret place; and your Father who sees in secret will reward you openly. And when you pray, do not use vain repetitions as the heathen do. For they think that they will be heard for their many words.

"Therefore do not be like them. For your Father knows the things you have need of before you ask Him. In this manner, therefore, pray:

Our Father in heaven,
Hallowed be Your name.
Your kingdom come.

Your will be done

On earth as it is in heaven.

Give us this day our daily bread.

And forgive us our debts,

As we forgive our debtors.

And do not lead us into temptation,

But deliver us from the evil one.

For Yours is the kingdom and the power and

the glory forever. Amen.

"For if you forgive men their trespasses, your heavenly Father will also forgive you. But if you do not forgive men their trespasses, neither will your Father forgive your trespasses."

MATTHEW 6:5–15

So Moses made haste and bowed his head toward the earth, and worshiped.

EXODUS 34:8

Then David said to all the assembly, "Now bless the Lord your God." So all the assembly blessed the Lord God of their fathers, and bowed their heads and prostrated themselves before the Lord and the king.

1 CHRONICLES 29:20

Now the acts of King David, first and last, indeed they are written in the book of Samuel the seer, in the book of Nathan the prophet, and in the book of Gad the seer, with all his reign and his might, and the events that happened to him, to Israel, and to all the kingdoms of the lands.

1 CHRONICLES 29:29–30

And Ezra blessed the LORD, the great God.

Then all the people answered, "Amen, Amen!" while lifting up their hands. And they bowed their heads and worshiped the LORD with their faces to the ground.

NEHEMIAH 8:6

Then King David went in and sat before the LORD; and he said: "Who am I, O Lord God? And what is my house, that You have brought me this far?"

1 CHRONICLES 17:16

And suddenly there came a sound from heaven, as of a rushing mighty wind, and it filled the whole house where they were sitting.

ACTS 2:2

And so it was, when Solomon had finished praying all this prayer and supplication to the LORD, that he arose from before the altar of the LORD, from kneeling on his knees with his hands spread up to heaven.

1 KINGS 8:54

For Solomon had made a bronze platform five cubits long, five cubits wide, and three cubits high, and had set it in the midst of the court; and he stood on it, knelt down on his knees before all the assembly of Israel, and spread out his hands toward heaven.

2 CHRONICLES 6:13

And when he had said these things, he knelt down and prayed with them all.

ACTS 20:36

Then Abram fell on his face, and God talked with him, saying: "As for Me, behold, My covenant is with you, and you shall be a father of many nations."

GENESIS 17:3–4

And Jehoshaphat bowed his head with his face to the ground, and all Judah and the inhabitants of Jerusalem bowed before the Lord, worshiping the Lord.

2 CHRONICLES 20:18

Now while Ezra was praying, and while he was confessing, weeping, and bowing down before the house of God, a very large assembly of men, women, and children gathered to him from Israel; for the people wept very bitterly.

EZRA 10:1

Like the appearance of a rainbow in a cloud on a rainy day, so was the appearance of the brightness all around it. This was the appearance of the likeness of the glory of the Lord.

EZEKIEL 1:28

Yet I heard the sound of his words; and while I heard the sound of his words I was in a deep sleep on my face, with my face to the ground.

DANIEL 10:9

And when the disciples heard it, they fell on their faces and were greatly afraid.

MATTHEW 17:6

The next day, as they went on their journey and drew near the city, Peter went up on the housetop to pray, about the sixth hour. Then he became very hungry and wanted to eat; but while they made ready, he fell into a trance.

ACTS 10:9–10

And when I saw Him, I fell at His feet as dead. But He laid His right hand on me, saying to me, "Do not be afraid; I am the First and the Last."

REVELATION 1:17

Then the king turned around and blessed the whole assembly of Israel, while all the assembly of Israel was standing. . . .

Then Solomon stood before the altar of the LORD in the presence of all the assembly of Israel, and spread out his hands toward heaven. . . .

Then he stood and blessed all the assembly of Israel with a loud voice, saying: "Blessed be the LORD, who has given rest to His people Israel, according to all that He promised. There has not failed one word of all His good promise, which He promised through His servant Moses. May the LORD our God be with us, as He was with our fathers. May He not leave us nor forsake us."

1 KINGS 8:14, 22, 55–57

Then Solomon stood before the altar of the LORD in the presence of all the assembly of Israel, and spread out his hands (for Solomon had made a bronze platform five cubits long, five cubits wide, and three cubits high, and had set it in the midst of the court; and he stood on it, knelt down on his knees before all the assembly of Israel, and spread out his hands toward heaven); and he said: "LORD God of Israel, there is no God in heaven or on earth like You, who keep Your covenant and mercy with Your servants who walk before You with all their hearts."

2 CHRONICLES 6:12–14

All the people saw the pillar of cloud standing at the tabernacle door, and all the people rose and worshiped, each man in his tent door.

EXODUS 33:10

"And when you pray, you shall not be like the hypocrites. For they love to pray standing in the synagogues and on the corners of the streets, that they may be seen by men. Assuredly, I say to you, they have their reward. But you, when you pray, go into your room, and when you have shut your door, pray to your Father who is in the secret place; and your Father who sees in secret will reward you openly. And when you pray, do not use vain repetitions as the heathen do. For they think that they will be heard for their many words.

"Therefore do not be like them. For your Father knows the things you have need of before you ask Him. In this manner, therefore, pray:

> Our Father in heaven,
> Hallowed be Your name.
> Your kingdom come.
> Your will be done
> On earth as it is in heaven.
> Give us this day our daily bread.
> And forgive us our debts,
> As we forgive our debtors.
> And do not lead us into temptation,
> But deliver us from the evil one.
> For Yours is the kingdom and the power and
> the glory forever. Amen.

"For if you forgive men their trespasses, your heavenly

Father will also forgive you. But if you do not forgive men their trespasses, neither will your Father forgive your trespasses."

MATTHEW 6:5–15

AGREEMENT IN PRAYER

Then God said: "No, Sarah your wife shall bear you a son, and you shall call his name Isaac; I will establish My covenant with him for an everlasting covenant, and with his descendants after him."

GENESIS 17:19

"For You said, 'I will surely treat you well, and make your descendants as the sand of the sea, which cannot be numbered for multitude.'"

GENESIS 32:12

"Remember Abraham, Isaac, and Israel, Your servants, to whom You swore by Your own self, and said to them, 'I will multiply your descendants as the stars of heaven; and all this land that I have spoken of I give to your descendants, and they shall inherit it forever.'"

EXODUS 32:13

And he said, "Listen, all you of Judah and you inhabitants of Jerusalem, and you, King Jehoshaphat! Thus says the LORD to you: 'Do not be afraid nor dismayed because of this great multitude, for the battle is not yours, but God's. Tomorrow go down against them. They will surely come up by the Ascent of Ziz, and you will find them at the end of the brook before the Wilderness of Jeruel. You will not need to fight in this battle. Position yourselves, stand still and see the salvation of the Lord, who is with you, O Judah and Jerusalem!' Do not fear or be dismayed; tomorrow go out against them, for the LORD is with you."

2 CHRONICLES 20:15–17

My covenant I will not break,
Nor alter the word that has gone out of My lips.

PSALM 89:34

For the LORD shall build up Zion;
He shall appear in His glory.
He shall regard the prayer of the destitute,
And shall not despise their prayer.

PSALM 102:16–17

"Incline your ear, and come to Me.
Hear, and your soul shall live;
And I will make an everlasting covenant
        with you—
The sure mercies of David."

ISAIAH 55:3

"For I, the LORD, love justice;
I hate robbery for burnt offering;
I will direct their work in truth,
And will make with them an everlasting
        covenant."

ISAIAH 61:8

"Behold, the days are coming, says the LORD, when I will make a new covenant with the house of Israel and with the house of Judah—not according to the covenant that I made with their fathers in the day that I took them by the hand to lead them out of the land of Egypt, My covenant which they broke, though I was a husband to them, says the LORD. But this is the covenant that I will make with the house of Israel after those days, says the LORD: I will put My law in their minds, and write it on their hearts; and I will be their God, and they shall be My people. No more

shall every man teach his neighbor, and every man
his brother, saying, 'Know the Lord,' for they all shall
know Me, from the least of them to the greatest of
them, says the Lord. For I will forgive their iniquity,
and their sin I will remember no more."

JEREMIAH 31:31–34

O my God, incline Your ear and hear; open Your eyes
and see our desolations, and the city which is called
by Your name; for we do not present our supplications before You because of our righteous deeds, but
because of Your great mercies. O Lord, hear! O Lord,
forgive! O Lord, listen and act! Do not delay for Your
own sake, my God, for Your city and Your people are
called by Your name.

DANIEL 9:18–19

"Again I say to you that if two of you agree on earth
concerning anything that they ask, it will be done for
them by My Father in heaven."

MATTHEW 18:19

Christ has redeemed us from the curse of the law, having become a curse for us (for it is written, "Cursed
is everyone who hangs on a tree"), that the blessing

of Abraham might come upon the Gentiles in Christ Jesus, that we might receive the promise of the Spirit through faith.

Brethren, I speak in the manner of men: Though it is only a man's covenant, yet if it is confirmed, no one annuls or adds to it. Now to Abraham and his Seed were the promises made. He does not say, "And to seeds," as of many, but as of one, "And to your Seed," who is Christ. And this I say, that the law, which was four hundred and thirty years later, cannot annul the covenant that was confirmed before by God in Christ, that it should make the promise of no effect. For if the inheritance is of the law, it is no longer of promise; but God gave it to Abraham by promise.

What purpose then does the law serve? It was added because of transgressions, till the Seed should come to whom the promise was made; and it was appointed through angels by the hand of a mediator. Now a mediator does not mediate for one only, but God is one.

Is the law then against the promises of God? Certainly not! For if there had been a law given which could have given life, truly righteousness would have been by the law. But the Scripture has confined all under sin, that the promise by faith in Jesus Christ might be given to those who believe. But before faith came, we were kept under guard by the law, kept for the faith which would afterward be revealed. Therefore the law was our tutor to bring us to Christ, that we might be justified by faith. But after faith has come, we are no longer under a tutor.

For you are all sons of God through faith in Christ Jesus. For as many of you as were baptized into Christ have put on Christ. There is neither Jew nor Greek, there is neither slave nor free, there is neither male nor female; for you are all one in Christ Jesus. And if you are Christ's, then you are Abraham's seed, and heirs according to the promise.

GALATIANS 3:13–29

But now He has obtained a more excellent ministry, inasmuch as He is also Mediator of a better covenant, which was established on better promises. . . .
For this is the covenant that I will make with the house of Israel after those days, says the LORD: I will put My laws in their mind and write them on their hearts; and I will be their God, and they shall be My people.

HEBREWS 8:6, 10

To the general assembly and church of the firstborn who are registered in heaven, to God the Judge of all, to the spirits of just men made perfect, to Jesus the Mediator of the new covenant, and to the blood of sprinkling that speaks better things than that of Abel.

See that you do not refuse Him who speaks. For if they did not escape who refused Him who spoke on earth, much more shall we not escape if we turn away from Him who speaks from heaven.

HEBREWS 12:23–25

Now may the God of peace who brought up our Lord Jesus from the dead, that great Shepherd of the sheep, through the blood of the everlasting covenant, make you complete in every good work to do His will, working in you what is well pleasing in His sight, through Jesus Christ, to whom be glory forever and ever. Amen.

HEBREWS 13:20–21

So he said, "I am Abraham's servant. The LORD has blessed my master greatly, and he has become great; and He has given him flocks and herds, silver and gold, male and female servants, and camels and donkeys. And Sarah my master's wife bore a son to my master when she was old; and to him he has given all that he has. Now my master made me swear, saying, 'You shall not take a wife for my son from the daughters of the Canaanites, in whose land I dwell; but you shall go to my father's house and to my family, and take a wife for my son.' And I said to my master, 'Perhaps the woman will not follow me.' But he said to me, 'The LORD, before whom I walk, will send His angel with you and prosper your way; and you shall take a wife for my son from my family and from my father's house.'"

GENESIS 24:34–40

"And he will turn
The hearts of the fathers to the children,
And the hearts of the children to their fathers,
Lest I come and strike the earth with a curse."

MALACHI 4:6

And the whole multitude of the people was praying outside at the hour of incense.

LUKE 1:10

Then fear came upon all, and they glorified God, saying, "A great prophet has risen up among us"; and, "God has visited His people."

LUKE 7:16

So when they heard that, they raised their voice to God with one accord and said: "Lord, You are God, who made heaven and earth and the sea, and all that is in them."

ACTS 4:24

So, when he had considered this, he came to the house of Mary, the mother of John whose surname was Mark, where many were gathered together praying.

ACTS 12:12

So Abraham prayed to God; and God healed Abimelech, his wife, and his female servants. Then they bore children; for the LORD had closed up all the wombs of the house of Abimelech because of Sarah, Abraham's wife.

GENESIS 20:17–18

Now Isaac pleaded with the LORD for his wife, because she was barren; and the LORD granted his plea, and Rebekah his wife conceived.

GENESIS 25:21

So the woman came and told her husband, saying, "A Man of God came to me, and His countenance was like the countenance of the Angel of God, very awesome; but I did not ask Him where He was from, and He did not tell me His name. And He said to me, 'Behold, you shall conceive and bear a son. Now drink no wine or similar drink, nor eat anything unclean, for the child shall be a Nazirite to God from the womb to the day of his death.'"

Then Manoah prayed to the LORD, and said, "O my Lord, please let the Man of God whom You sent come to us again and teach us what we shall do for the child who will be born." . . .

So the Angel of the LORD said to Manoah, "Of all that I said to the woman let her be careful." . . .

So the woman bore a son and called his name Samson; and the child grew, and the LORD blessed him.

JUDGES 13:6–8, 13, 24

When we had come to the end of those days, we departed and went on our way; and they all accompanied us, with wives and children, till we were out of the city. And we knelt down on the shore and prayed.

ACTS 21:5

A devout man and one who feared God with all his household, who gave alms generously to the people, and prayed to God always. . . .

So Cornelius said, "Four days ago I was fasting until this hour; and at the ninth hour I prayed in my house, and behold, a man stood before me in bright clothing, and said, 'Cornelius, your prayer has been heard, and your alms are remembered in the sight of God.'"

ACTS 10:2, 30–31

And she was in bitterness of soul, and prayed to the LORD and wept in anguish. Then she made a vow and said, "O LORD of hosts, if You will indeed look on the affliction of Your maidservant and remember me, and not forget Your maidservant, but will give Your maidservant a male child, then I will give him to the LORD all the days of his life, and no razor shall come upon his head."

And it happened, as she continued praying before the LORD, that Eli watched her mouth. Now Hannah spoke in her heart; only her lips moved, but her voice was not heard. Therefore Eli thought she was drunk. So Eli said to her, "How long will you be drunk? Put your wine away from you!"

But Hannah answered and said, "No, my lord, I am a woman of sorrowful spirit. I have drunk neither wine nor intoxicating drink, but have poured out my soul before the LORD. Do not consider your maidservant a wicked woman, for out of the abundance of my complaint and grief I have spoken until now."

Then Eli answered and said, "Go in peace, and the God of Israel grant your petition which you have asked of Him."

And she said, "Let your maidservant find favor in your sight." So the woman went her way and ate, and her face was no longer sad.

Then they rose early in the morning and worshiped before the LORD, and returned and came to their house at Ramah. And Elkanah knew Hannah his wife, and the LORD remembered her. So it came to pass in the process of time that Hannah conceived and bore a son, and called his name Samuel, saying, "Because I have asked for him from the LORD."

1 SAMUEL 1:10–20, 26–28

But the angel said to him, "Do not be afraid, Zacharias, for your prayer is heard; and your wife Elizabeth will bear you a son, and you shall call his name John."

LUKE 1:13

Blessed is the nation whose God is the LORD,
The people He has chosen as His own
    inheritance.

PSALM 33:12

As I urged you when I went into Macedonia—remain
in Ephesus that you may charge some that they teach
no other doctrine. . . . But we know that the law is
good if one uses it lawfully.

1 TIMOTHY 1:3, 8

Therefore I exhort first of all that supplications,
prayers, intercessions, and giving of thanks be made
for all men, for kings and all who are in authority,
that we may lead a quiet and peaceable life in all god-
liness and reverence. For this is good and acceptable
in the sight of God our Savior.

1 TIMOTHY 2:1–3

PRAYING THE PSALMS

God has promised that His Word shall not return void. When we pray back to God through His Word, He has promised to provide His provision, protection, strength, greatness, and so much more. We belong to the Father and we are His children. He wants the best for us and through His Word we are blessed. We only need to come to the Lord with open hearts and minds and receive His Word. "The LORD is my shepherd; I shall not want." Come to the Lord often, praying the psalms and lifting up God's words, and He will bless you immensely.

GOD'S PROVISION

Blessed is the man
> Who walks not in the counsel of the ungodly,
> Nor stands in the path of sinners,
> Nor sits in the seat of the scornful;
> But his delight is in the law of the LORD,

And in His law he meditates day and night.
He shall be like a tree
Planted by the rivers of water,
That brings forth its fruit in its season,
Whose leaf also shall not wither;
And whatever he does shall prosper.

The ungodly are not so,
But are like the chaff which the wind
        drives away.
Therefore the ungodly shall not stand in the
        judgment,
Nor sinners in the congregation of the
        righteous.

For the LORD knows the way of the righteous,
But the way of the ungodly shall perish.

PSALM 1

GOD'S PROTECTION

Give ear to my words, O LORD,
        Consider my meditation.
        Give heed to the voice of my cry,
        My King and my God,
        For to You I will pray.

My voice You shall hear in the morning,
O Lord;
In the morning I will direct it to You,
And I will look up.

For You are not a God who takes pleasure in
wickedness,
Nor shall evil dwell with You.
The boastful shall not stand in Your sight;
You hate all workers of iniquity.
You shall destroy those who speak falsehood;
The Lord abhors the bloodthirsty and
deceitful man.

But as for me, I will come into Your house in
the multitude of Your mercy;
In fear of You I will worship toward Your holy
temple.
Lead me, O Lord, in Your righteousness
because of my enemies;
Make Your way straight before my face.

For there is no faithfulness in their mouth;
Their inward part is destruction;
Their throat is an open tomb;
They flatter with their tongue.

Pronounce them guilty, O God!
Let them fall by their own counsels;
Cast them out in the multitude of their
transgressions,
For they have rebelled against You.

But let all those rejoice who put their trust
in You;
Let them ever shout for joy, because You
defend them;
Let those also who love Your name
Be joyful in You.
For You, O LORD, will bless the righteous;
With favor You will surround him as with a
shield.

PSALM 5

PRAISE TO THE LORD

O LORD, our Lord,
How excellent is Your name in all the earth,
Who have set Your glory above the heavens!

Out of the mouth of babes and nursing infants
You have ordained strength,
Because of Your enemies,

That You may silence the enemy and the
    avenger.

When I consider Your heavens, the work of
    Your fingers,
The moon and the stars, which You have
    ordained,
What is man that You are mindful of him,
And the son of man that You visit him?
For You have made him a little lower than the
    angels,
And You have crowned him with glory and
    honor.

You have made him to have dominion over the
    works of Your hands;
You have put all things under his feet,
All sheep and oxen—
Even the beasts of the field,
The birds of the air,
And the fish of the sea
That pass through the paths of the seas.

O Lord, our Lord,
How excellent is Your name in all the earth!

PSALM 8

OUR PRESERVATION

Preserve me, O God, for in You I put my trust.

O my soul, you have said to the LORD,
"You are my Lord,
My goodness is nothing apart from You."
As for the saints who are on the earth,
"They are the excellent ones, in whom is all my
     delight."

Their sorrows shall be multiplied who hasten
     after another god;
Their drink offerings of blood I will not offer,
Nor take up their names on my lips.

O LORD, You are the portion of my inheritance
     and my cup;
You maintain my lot.
The lines have fallen to me in pleasant places;
Yes, I have a good inheritance.

I will bless the LORD who has given me counsel;
My heart also instructs me in the night seasons.
I have set the LORD always before me;
Because He is at my right hand I shall not be
     moved.

Therefore my heart is glad, and my glory
    rejoices;
My flesh also will rest in hope.
For You will not leave my soul in Sheol,
Nor will You allow Your Holy One to see
    corruption.
You will show me the path of life;
In Your presence is fullness of joy;
At Your right hand are pleasures forevermore.

PSALM 16

OUR COMFORT

The LORD is my shepherd;
    I shall not want.
    He makes me to lie down in green pastures;
    He leads me beside the still waters.
    He restores my soul;
    He leads me in the paths of righteousness
    For His name's sake.

    Yea, though I walk through the valley of the
        shadow of death,
    I will fear no evil;
    For You are with me;

Your rod and Your staff, they comfort me.

You prepare a table before me in the presence of
      my enemies;
You anoint my head with oil;
My cup runs over.
Surely goodness and mercy shall follow me
All the days of my life;
And I will dwell in the house of the LORD
Forever.

PSALM 23

GOD'S SOVEREIGNTY

The earth is the LORD's, and all its fullness,
     The world and those who dwell therein.
     For He has founded it upon the seas,
     And established it upon the waters.

     Who may ascend into the hill of the LORD?
     Or who may stand in His holy place?
     He who has clean hands and a pure heart,
     Who has not lifted up his soul to an idol,
     Nor sworn deceitfully.
     He shall receive blessing from the LORD,

And righteousness from the God of his
    salvation.
This is Jacob, the generation of those who
    seek Him,
Who seek Your face. *Selah*

Lift up your heads, O you gates!
And be lifted up, you everlasting doors!
And the King of glory shall come in.
Who is this King of glory?
The Lord strong and mighty,
The Lord mighty in battle.
Lift up your heads, O you gates!
Lift up, you everlasting doors!
And the King of glory shall come in.
Who is this King of glory?
The Lord of hosts,
He is the King of glory.

PSALM 24

GOD'S STRENGTH

The Lord is my light and my salvation;
    Whom shall I fear?
    The Lord is the strength of my life;

Of whom shall I be afraid?
When the wicked came against me
To eat up my flesh,
My enemies and foes,
They stumbled and fell.
Though an army may encamp against me,
My heart shall not fear;
Though war may rise against me,
In this I will be confident.

One thing I have desired of the LORD,
That will I seek:
That I may dwell in the house of the LORD
All the days of my life,
To behold the beauty of the LORD,
And to inquire in His temple.
For in the time of trouble
He shall hide me in His pavilion;
In the secret place of His tabernacle
He shall hide me;
He shall set me high upon a rock.

And now my head shall be lifted up above my
        enemies all around me;
Therefore I will offer sacrifices of joy in His
        tabernacle;

I will sing, yes, I will sing praises to the Lord.

Hear, O Lord, when I cry with my voice!
Have mercy also upon me, and answer me.
When You said, "Seek My face,"
My heart said to You, "Your face, Lord, I
    will seek."
Do not hide Your face from me;
Do not turn Your servant away in anger;
You have been my help;
Do not leave me nor forsake me,
O God of my salvation.
When my father and my mother forsake me,
Then the Lord will take care of me.

Teach me Your way, O Lord,
And lead me in a smooth path, because of my
    enemies.
Do not deliver me to the will of my adversaries;
For false witnesses have risen against me,
And such as breathe out violence.
I would have lost heart, unless I had believed
That I would see the goodness of the Lord
In the land of the living.

Wait on the Lord;

Be of good courage,

And He shall strengthen your heart;

Wait, I say, on the LORD!

PSALM 27

OUR PROTECTION

Plead my cause, O LORD, with those who strive
with me;

Fight against those who fight against me.

Take hold of shield and buckler,

And stand up for my help.

Also draw out the spear,

And stop those who pursue me.

Say to my soul,

"I am your salvation."

Let those be put to shame and brought to
dishonor

Who seek after my life;

Let those be turned back and brought to
confusion

Who plot my hurt.

Let them be like chaff before the wind,

And let the angel of the LORD chase them.

Let their way be dark and slippery,
And let the angel of the Lord pursue them.
For without cause they have hidden their net for
     me in a pit,
Which they have dug without cause for my life.
Let destruction come upon him unexpectedly,
And let his net that he has hidden catch
     himself;
Into that very destruction let him fall.

And my soul shall be joyful in the Lord;
It shall rejoice in His salvation.
All my bones shall say,
"Lord, who is like You,
Delivering the poor from him who is too strong
     for him,
Yes, the poor and the needy from him who
     plunders him?"

Fierce witnesses rise up;
They ask me things that I do not know.
They reward me evil for good,
To the sorrow of my soul.
But as for me, when they were sick,
My clothing was sackcloth;
I humbled myself with fasting;

And my prayer would return to my own heart.
I paced about as though he were my friend or
    brother;
I bowed down heavily, as one who mourns for
    his mother.

But in my adversity they rejoiced
And gathered together;
Attackers gathered against me,
And I did not know it;
They tore at me and did not cease;
With ungodly mockers at feasts
They gnashed at me with their teeth.

Lord, how long will You look on?
Rescue me from their destructions,
My precious life from the lions.
I will give You thanks in the great assembly;
I will praise You among many people.

Let them not rejoice over me who are
    wrongfully my enemies;
Nor let them wink with the eye who hate me
    without a cause.
For they do not speak peace,
But they devise deceitful matters

Against the quiet ones in the land.
They also opened their mouth wide against me,
And said, "Aha, aha!
Our eyes have seen it."

This You have seen, O Lord;
Do not keep silence.
O Lord, do not be far from me.
Stir up Yourself, and awake to my vindication,
To my cause, my God and my Lord.
Vindicate me, O Lord my God, according to
        Your righteousness;
And let them not rejoice over me.
Let them not say in their hearts, "Ah, so we
        would have it!"
Let them not say, "We have swallowed him up."

Let them be ashamed and brought to mutual
        confusion
Who rejoice at my hurt;
Let them be clothed with shame and dishonor
Who exalt themselves against me.

Let them shout for joy and be glad,
Who favor my righteous cause;
And let them say continually,

"Let the LORD be magnified,
Who has pleasure in the prosperity of His
    servant."
And my tongue shall speak of Your
    righteousness
And of Your praise all the day long.

PSALM 35

GOD'S COMPASSION

Blessed is he who considers the poor;
    The LORD will deliver him in time of trouble.
    The LORD will preserve him and keep him
        alive,
    And he will be blessed on the earth;
    You will not deliver him to the will of his
        enemies.
    The LORD will strengthen him on his bed of
        illness;
    You will sustain him on his sickbed.

I said, "LORD, be merciful to me;
Heal my soul, for I have sinned against You."
My enemies speak evil of me:
"When will he die, and his name perish?"

And if he comes to see me, he speaks lies;
His heart gathers iniquity to itself;
When he goes out, he tells it.

All who hate me whisper together against me;
Against me they devise my hurt.
"An evil disease," they say, "clings to him.
And now that he lies down, he will rise up
      no more."
Even my own familiar friend in whom I trusted,
Who ate my bread,
Has lifted up his heel against me.

But You, O Lord, be merciful to me, and raise
      me up,
That I may repay them.
By this I know that You are well pleased
      with me,
Because my enemy does not triumph over me.
As for me, You uphold me in my integrity,
And set me before Your face forever.

Blessed be the Lord God of Israel
From everlasting to everlasting!
Amen and Amen.

PSALM 41

OUR YEARNING FOR THE LORD

As the deer pants for the water brooks,
 So pants my soul for You, O God.
 My soul thirsts for God, for the living God.
 When shall I come and appear before God?
 My tears have been my food day and night,
 While they continually say to me,
 "Where is your God?"

 When I remember these things,
 I pour out my soul within me.
 For I used to go with the multitude;
 I went with them to the house of God,
 With the voice of joy and praise,
 With a multitude that kept a pilgrim feast.

 Why are you cast down, O my soul?
 And why are you disquieted within me?
 Hope in God, for I shall yet praise Him
 For the help of His countenance.

 O my God, my soul is cast down within me;
 Therefore I will remember You from the land of
  the Jordan,
 And from the heights of Hermon,

From the Hill Mizar.
Deep calls unto deep at the noise of Your
      waterfalls;
All Your waves and billows have gone over me.
The LORD will command His lovingkindness in
      the daytime,
And in the night His song shall be with me—
A prayer to the God of my life.

I will say to God my Rock,
"Why have You forgotten me?
Why do I go mourning because of the
      oppression of the enemy?"
As with a breaking of my bones,
My enemies reproach me,
While they say to me all day long,
"Where is your God?"

Why are you cast down, O my soul?
And why are you disquieted within me?
Hope in God;
For I shall yet praise Him,
The help of my countenance and my God.

PSALM 42

GOD'S POWER, PRESENCE, AND PEACE

God is our refuge and strength,
>A very present help in trouble.
>Therefore we will not fear,
>Even though the earth be removed,
>And though the mountains be carried into the
>>midst of the sea;
>Though its waters roar and be troubled,
>Though the mountains shake with its swelling.
>>*Selah*

>There is a river whose streams shall make glad
>>the city of God,
>The holy place of the tabernacle of the
>>Most High.
>God is in the midst of her, she shall not be
>>moved;
>God shall help her, just at the break of dawn.
>The nations raged, the kingdoms were moved;
>He uttered His voice, the earth melted.

>The LORD of hosts is with us;
>The God of Jacob is our refuge. *Selah*

Come, behold the works of the LORD,
Who has made desolations in the earth.
He makes wars cease to the end of the earth;
He breaks the bow and cuts the spear in two;
He burns the chariot in the fire.

Be still, and know that I am God;
I will be exalted among the nations,
I will be exalted in the earth!

The LORD of hosts is with us;
The God of Jacob is our refuge. *Selah*

PSALM 46

GOD'S FORGIVENESS

Have mercy upon me, O God,
According to Your lovingkindness;
According to the multitude of Your tender
mercies,
Blot out my transgressions.
Wash me thoroughly from my iniquity,
And cleanse me from my sin.

For I acknowledge my transgressions,
And my sin is always before me.

Against You, You only, have I sinned,
And done this evil in Your sight—
That You may be found just when You speak,
And blameless when You judge.

Behold, I was brought forth in iniquity,
And in sin my mother conceived me.
Behold, You desire truth in the inward parts,
And in the hidden part You will make me to
      know wisdom.

Purge me with hyssop, and I shall be clean;
Wash me, and I shall be whiter than snow.
Make me hear joy and gladness,
That the bones You have broken may rejoice.
Hide Your face from my sins,
And blot out all my iniquities.

Create in me a clean heart, O God,
And renew a steadfast spirit within me.
Do not cast me away from Your presence,
And do not take Your Holy Spirit from me.

Restore to me the joy of Your salvation,
And uphold me by Your generous Spirit.
Then I will teach transgressors Your ways,
And sinners shall be converted to You.

Deliver me from the guilt of bloodshed, O God,
The God of my salvation,
And my tongue shall sing aloud of Your
righteousness.
O Lord, open my lips,
And my mouth shall show forth Your praise.
For You do not desire sacrifice, or else I would
give it;
You do not delight in burnt offering.
The sacrifices of God are a broken spirit,
A broken and a contrite heart—
These, O God, You will not despise.

Do good in Your good pleasure to Zion;
Build the walls of Jerusalem.
Then You shall be pleased with the sacrifices of
righteousness,
With burnt offering and whole burnt offering;
Then they shall offer bulls on Your altar.

PSALM 51

OUR PETITIONS

Lord, You have been our dwelling place in all
generations.

Before the mountains were brought forth,
Or ever You had formed the earth and the
world,
Even from everlasting to everlasting, You
are God.

You turn man to destruction,
And say, "Return, O children of men."
For a thousand years in Your sight
Are like yesterday when it is past,
And like a watch in the night.
You carry them away like a flood;
They are like a sleep.
In the morning they are like grass which
grows up:
In the morning it flourishes and grows up;
In the evening it is cut down and withers.

For we have been consumed by Your anger,
And by Your wrath we are terrified.
You have set our iniquities before You,
Our secret sins in the light of Your countenance.
For all our days have passed away in Your
wrath;
We finish our years like a sigh.
The days of our lives are seventy years;

And if by reason of strength they are eighty
    years,
Yet their boast is only labor and sorrow;
For it is soon cut off, and we fly away.
Who knows the power of Your anger?
For as the fear of You, so is Your wrath.
So teach us to number our days,
That we may gain a heart of wisdom.

Return, O Lord!
How long?
And have compassion on Your servants.
Oh, satisfy us early with Your mercy,
That we may rejoice and be glad all our days!
Make us glad according to the days in which
    You have afflicted us,
The years in which we have seen evil.
Let Your work appear to Your servants,
And Your glory to their children.
And let the beauty of the Lord our God be
    upon us,
And establish the work of our hands for us;
Yes, establish the work of our hands.

PSALM 90

GOD'S GREATNESS

Hear my prayer, O LORD,
>And let my cry come to You.
>Do not hide Your face from me in the day of my
>>trouble;
>Incline Your ear to me;
>In the day that I call, answer me speedily.

>For my days are consumed like smoke,
>And my bones are burned like a hearth.
>My heart is stricken and withered like grass,
>So that I forget to eat my bread.
>Because of the sound of my groaning
>My bones cling to my skin.
>I am like a pelican of the wilderness;
>I am like an owl of the desert.
>I lie awake,
>And am like a sparrow alone on the housetop.

>My enemies reproach me all day long;
>Those who deride me swear an oath against me.
>For I have eaten ashes like bread,
>And mingled my drink with weeping,
>Because of Your indignation and Your wrath;
>For You have lifted me up and cast me away.

My days are like a shadow that lengthens,
And I wither away like grass.

But You, O Lord, shall endure forever,
And the remembrance of Your name to all
        generations.
You will arise and have mercy on Zion;
For the time to favor her,
Yes, the set time, has come.
For Your servants take pleasure in her stones,
And show favor to her dust.
So the nations shall fear the name of the Lord,
And all the kings of the earth Your glory.
For the Lord shall build up Zion;
He shall appear in His glory.
He shall regard the prayer of the destitute,
And shall not despise their prayer.

This will be written for the generation to come,
That a people yet to be created may praise
        the Lord.
For He looked down from the height of His
        sanctuary;
From heaven the Lord viewed the earth,
To hear the groaning of the prisoner,
To release those appointed to death,

To declare the name of the LORD in Zion,
And His praise in Jerusalem,
When the peoples are gathered together,
And the kingdoms, to serve the LORD.

He weakened my strength in the way;
He shortened my days.
I said, "O my God,
Do not take me away in the midst of my days;
Your years are throughout all generations.
Of old You laid the foundation of the earth,
And the heavens are the work of Your hands.
They will perish, but You will endure;
Yes, they will all grow old like a garment;
Like a cloak You will change them,
And they will be changed.
But You are the same,
And Your years will have no end.
The children of Your servants will continue,
And their descendants will be established
        before You."

PSALM 102

Bless the LORD, O my soul;
And all that is within me, bless His holy name!

Bless the LORD, O my soul,
And forget not all His benefits:
Who forgives all your iniquities,
Who heals all your diseases,
Who redeems your life from destruction,
Who crowns you with lovingkindness and
      tender mercies,
Who satisfies your mouth with good things,
So that your youth is renewed like the eagle's.

The LORD executes righteousness
And justice for all who are oppressed.
He made known His ways to Moses,
His acts to the children of Israel.
The LORD is merciful and gracious,
Slow to anger, and abounding in mercy.
He will not always strive with us,
Nor will He keep His anger forever.
He has not dealt with us according to our sins,
Nor punished us according to our iniquities.

For as the heavens are high above the earth,
So great is His mercy toward those who
      fear Him;
As far as the east is from the west,

So far has He removed our transgressions
    from us.
As a father pities his children,
So the LORD pities those who fear Him.
For He knows our frame;
He remembers that we are dust.

As for man, his days are like grass;
As a flower of the field, so he flourishes.
For the wind passes over it, and it is gone,
And its place remembers it no more.
But the mercy of the LORD is from everlasting
    to everlasting
On those who fear Him,
And His righteousness to children's children,
To such as keep His covenant,
And to those who remember His
    commandments to do them.

The LORD has established His throne in heaven,
And His kingdom rules over all.

Bless the LORD, you His angels,
Who excel in strength, who do His word,
Heeding the voice of His word.
Bless the LORD, all you His hosts,

You ministers of His, who do His pleasure.
Bless the Lord, all His works,
In all places of His dominion.

Bless the Lord, O my soul!

PSALM 103

Oh, give thanks to the Lord!
Call upon His name;
Make known His deeds among the peoples!
Sing to Him, sing psalms to Him;
Talk of all His wondrous works!
Glory in His holy name;
Let the hearts of those rejoice who seek
        the Lord!
Seek the Lord and His strength;
Seek His face evermore!
Remember His marvelous works which He
        has done,
His wonders, and the judgments of His mouth,
O seed of Abraham His servant,
You children of Jacob, His chosen ones!

He is the Lord our God;
His judgments are in all the earth.
He remembers His covenant forever,

The word which He commanded, for a
          thousand generations,
The covenant which He made with Abraham,
And His oath to Isaac,
And confirmed it to Jacob for a statute,
To Israel as an everlasting covenant,
Saying, "To you I will give the land of Canaan
As the allotment of your inheritance,"
When they were few in number,
Indeed very few, and strangers in it.

When they went from one nation to another,
From one kingdom to another people,
He permitted no one to do them wrong;
Yes, He rebuked kings for their sakes,
Saying, "Do not touch My anointed ones,
And do My prophets no harm."

Moreover He called for a famine in the land;
He destroyed all the provision of bread.
He sent a man before them—
Joseph—who was sold as a slave.
They hurt his feet with fetters,
He was laid in irons.
Until the time that his word came to pass,
The word of the LORD tested him.

The king sent and released him,
The ruler of the people let him go free.
He made him lord of his house,
And ruler of all his possessions,
To bind his princes at his pleasure,
And teach his elders wisdom.

Israel also came into Egypt,
And Jacob dwelt in the land of Ham.
He increased His people greatly,
And made them stronger than their enemies.
He turned their heart to hate His people,
To deal craftily with His servants.

He sent Moses His servant,
And Aaron whom He had chosen.
They performed His signs among them,
And wonders in the land of Ham.
He sent darkness, and made it dark;
And they did not rebel against His word.
He turned their waters into blood,
And killed their fish.
Their land abounded with frogs,
Even in the chambers of their kings.
He spoke, and there came swarms of flies,
And lice in all their territory.

He gave them hail for rain,
And flaming fire in their land.
He struck their vines also, and their fig trees,
And splintered the trees of their territory.
He spoke, and locusts came,
Young locusts without number,
And ate up all the vegetation in their land,
And devoured the fruit of their ground.
He also destroyed all the firstborn in their land,
The first of all their strength.

He also brought them out with silver and gold,
And there was none feeble among His tribes.
Egypt was glad when they departed,
For the fear of them had fallen upon them.
He spread a cloud for a covering,
And fire to give light in the night.
The people asked, and He brought quail,
And satisfied them with the bread of heaven.
He opened the rock, and water gushed out;
It ran in the dry places like a river.

For He remembered His holy promise,
And Abraham His servant.
He brought out His people with joy,
His chosen ones with gladness.

He gave them the lands of the Gentiles,
And they inherited the labor of the nations,
That they might observe His statutes
And keep His laws.
Praise the LORD!

PSALM 105

GOD'S MERCY

Oh, give thanks to the LORD, for He is good!
For His mercy endures forever.
Let the redeemed of the LORD say so,
Whom He has redeemed from the hand of the
    enemy,
And gathered out of the lands,
From the east and from the west,
From the north and from the south.

They wandered in the wilderness in a
    desolate way;
They found no city to dwell in.
Hungry and thirsty,
Their soul fainted in them.
Then they cried out to the LORD in their
    trouble,

And He delivered them out of their distresses.
And He led them forth by the right way,
That they might go to a city for a dwelling place.
Oh, that men would give thanks to the LORD for
     His goodness,
And for His wonderful works to the children
     of men!
For He satisfies the longing soul,
And fills the hungry soul with goodness.

Those who sat in darkness and in the shadow
     of death,
Bound in affliction and irons—
Because they rebelled against the words of God,
And despised the counsel of the Most High,
Therefore He brought down their heart with
     labor;
They fell down, and there was none to help.
Then they cried out to the LORD in their
     trouble,
And He saved them out of their distresses.
He brought them out of darkness and the
     shadow of death,
And broke their chains in pieces.

Oh, that men would give thanks to the LORD for
His goodness,
And for His wonderful works to the children
of men!
For He has broken the gates of bronze,
And cut the bars of iron in two.

Fools, because of their transgression,
And because of their iniquities, were afflicted.
Their soul abhorred all manner of food,
And they drew near to the gates of death.
Then they cried out to the LORD in their
trouble,
And He saved them out of their distresses.
He sent His word and healed them,
And delivered them from their destructions.
Oh, that men would give thanks to the LORD for
His goodness,
And for His wonderful works to the children
of men!
Let them sacrifice the sacrifices of
thanksgiving,
And declare His works with rejoicing.

Those who go down to the sea in ships,
Who do business on great waters,

They see the works of the LORD,
And His wonders in the deep.
For He commands and raises the stormy wind,
Which lifts up the waves of the sea.
They mount up to the heavens,
They go down again to the depths;
Their soul melts because of trouble.
They reel to and fro, and stagger like a
      drunken man,
And are at their wits' end.
Then they cry out to the LORD in their trouble,
And He brings them out of their distresses.
He calms the storm,
So that its waves are still.
Then they are glad because they are quiet;
So He guides them to their desired haven.
Oh, that men would give thanks to the LORD for
      His goodness,
And for His wonderful works to the children
      of men!
Let them exalt Him also in the assembly of the
      people,
And praise Him in the company of the elders.

He turns rivers into a wilderness,

And the watersprings into dry ground;
A fruitful land into barrenness,
For the wickedness of those who dwell in it.
He turns a wilderness into pools of water,
And dry land into watersprings.
There He makes the hungry dwell,
That they may establish a city for a dwelling
      place,
And sow fields and plant vineyards,
That they may yield a fruitful harvest.
He also blesses them, and they multiply greatly;
And He does not let their cattle decrease.

When they are diminished and brought low
Through oppression, affliction, and sorrow,
He pours contempt on princes,
And causes them to wander in the wilderness
      where there is no way;
Yet He sets the poor on high, far from affliction,
And makes their families like a flock.
The righteous see it and rejoice,
And all iniquity stops its mouth.

Whoever is wise will observe these things,

And they will understand the lovingkindness of
the Lord.

PSALM 107

GOD'S PURITY

The heavens declare the glory of God;
    And the firmament shows His handiwork.
    Day unto day utters speech,
    And night unto night reveals knowledge.
    There is no speech nor language
    Where their voice is not heard.
    Their line has gone out through all the earth,
    And their words to the end of the world.

    In them He has set a tabernacle for the sun,
    Which is like a bridegroom coming out of his
        chamber,
    And rejoices like a strong man to run its race.
    Its rising is from one end of heaven,
    And its circuit to the other end;
    And there is nothing hidden from its heat.

    The law of the Lord is perfect, converting
        the soul;

The testimony of the LORD is sure, making wise
the simple;
The statutes of the LORD are right, rejoicing the
heart;
The commandment of the LORD is pure,
enlightening the eyes;
The fear of the LORD is clean, enduring forever;
The judgments of the LORD are true and
righteous altogether.
More to be desired are they than gold,
Yea, than much fine gold;
Sweeter also than honey and the honeycomb.
Moreover by them Your servant is warned,
And in keeping them there is great reward.

Who can understand his errors?
Cleanse me from secret faults.
Keep back Your servant also from
presumptuous sins;
Let them not have dominion over me.
Then I shall be blameless,
And I shall be innocent of great transgression.

Let the words of my mouth and the meditation
of my heart
Be acceptable in Your sight,

O Lord, my strength and my Redeemer.

PSALM 19

OUR PURITY

Who walk in the law of the Lord!
Blessed are those who keep His testimonies,
Who seek Him with the whole heart!
They also do no iniquity;
They walk in His ways.
You have commanded us
To keep Your precepts diligently.
Oh, that my ways were directed
To keep Your statutes!
Then I would not be ashamed,
When I look into all Your commandments.
I will praise You with uprightness of heart,
When I learn Your righteous judgments.
I will keep Your statutes;
Oh, do not forsake me utterly!

How can a young man cleanse his way?
By taking heed according to Your word.
With my whole heart I have sought You;

Oh, let me not wander from Your
    commandments!
Your word I have hidden in my heart,
That I might not sin against You.
Blessed are You, O LORD!
Teach me Your statutes.
With my lips I have declared
All the judgments of Your mouth.
I have rejoiced in the way of Your testimonies,
As much as in all riches.
I will meditate on Your precepts,
And contemplate Your ways.
I will delight myself in Your statutes;
I will not forget Your word.

Deal bountifully with Your servant,
That I may live and keep Your word.
Open my eyes, that I may see
Wondrous things from Your law.
I am a stranger in the earth;
Do not hide Your commandments from me.
My soul breaks with longing
For Your judgments at all times.
You rebuke the proud—the cursed,
Who stray from Your commandments.

Remove from me reproach and contempt,
For I have kept Your testimonies.
Princes also sit and speak against me,
But Your servant meditates on Your statutes.
Your testimonies also are my delight
And my counselors.

My soul clings to the dust;
Revive me according to Your word.
I have declared my ways, and You answered me;
Teach me Your statutes.
Make me understand the way of Your precepts;
So shall I meditate on Your wonderful works.
My soul melts from heaviness;
Strengthen me according to Your word.
Remove from me the way of lying,
And grant me Your law graciously.
I have chosen the way of truth;
Your judgments I have laid before me.
I cling to Your testimonies;
O Lord, do not put me to shame!
I will run the course of Your commandments,
For You shall enlarge my heart.

Teach me, O Lord, the way of Your statutes,
And I shall keep it to the end.

Give me understanding, and I shall keep
    Your law;
Indeed, I shall observe it with my whole heart.
Make me walk in the path of Your
    commandments,
For I delight in it.
Incline my heart to Your testimonies,
And not to covetousness.
Turn away my eyes from looking at worthless
    things,
And revive me in Your way.
Establish Your word to Your servant,
Who is devoted to fearing You.
Turn away my reproach which I dread,
For Your judgments are good.
Behold, I long for Your precepts;
Revive me in Your righteousness.

PSALM 119:1–40

ABOUT THE AUTHOR

Jack Countryman is the founder of JCountryman® Gift Books and the recipient of the Evangelical Christian Publishers Association Jordan Lifetime Achievement Award. Over the past thirty years, he has developed bestselling gift books such as *God's Promises® for Your Every Need* and *The Red Letter Words of Jesus*. Countryman's books have sold more than 27 million copies.